Naff Motors

The author Tony Davis has written about cars, on and off, for twenty years. He has driven some of the fastest, most expensive and most impressive vehicles ever built, yet retains a bizarre fascination with those at the other end of the spectrum, those created by designers and engineers who, as he puts it, 'think a *tour de force* is a bicycle race'.

Naff
Motors

101 Automotive Lemons
TONY DAVIS

Published by Century in 2006

3 5 7 9 10 8 6 4 2

Copyright © Tony Davis 2006

Tony Davis has asserted his right under the Copyright, Designs
and Patents Act, 1988 to be identified as the author of this work

First published in the United Kingdom in 2006 by Century
The Random House Group Limited
20 Vauxhall Bridge Road, London SW1V 2SA

Random House Australia (Pty) Limited
20 Alfred Street, Milsons Point, Sydney, New South Wales 2061, Australia

Random House New Zealand Limited
18 Poland Road, Glenfield, Auckland 10, New Zealand

Random House (Pty) Limited
Isle of Houghton, Corner of Boundary Road & Carse O'Gowrie,
Houghton 2198, South Africa

Random House Publishers India Private Limited
301 World Trade Tower, Hotel Intercontinental Grand Complex,
Barakhamba Lane, New Delhi 110 001, India

The Random House Group Limited Reg. No. 954009

www.randomhouse.co.uk

A CIP catalogue record for this book is available from the British Library

Papers used by Random House are natural, recyclable products made from wood
grown in sustainable forests. The manufacturing processes conform to the
environmental regulations of the country of origin

ISBN 1846050642
ISBN 9781846050640 (from Jan 2007)

Design/make up by Roger Walker

Printed and bound in Germany by
GGP Media GmbH, Pößneck

Contents

Acknowledgements

Many thanks to Carolyn Walsh, Pedr Davis, Jude McGee, Jessica Dettmann, Tim Vaughan, Claude Ludi, Joshua Dowling, Alistair Kennedy, Mike Toten, Andy Auchterlonie, Fred Diwell, Phil Scott and Timothy Andrews.

Introduction: Worst Things First

Most cars are fundamentally good. They look inoffensive, they go well, they are safe, reliable, and durable. And they sell in respectable numbers, returning an acceptable profit to the company that built them. Boring or what?

Naff motors – the dogs, lemons and automotive atrocities of the car world – are a different thing entirely. Few things in the world provide such a fascinating window into human daring and individuality. After all, there's really only one way to make a good car: with talented people doing things sensibly. There are, however, a million ways to produce a bad one, and no two car companies stuff things up in quite the same way.

The possibilities are almost endless: you can start with a bad idea, but execute it adequately (the Volvo 760); you can start with an adequate idea, but execute it badly (the Triumph Stag). Perhaps most interestingly of all, you can start with a ludicrous notion and, from there, take the wrong path at every fork along the bumpy road.

Perhaps the best example of this extreme and exalted category is the Zeta, from South Australian washing-machine manufacturer Lightburn. Although the brochure boasted that the Zeta was handsome, the photo made the opposite immediately obvious. And although the gushing spiel blurted on and on *and on and on* about a vehicle that cleverly combined the benefits of a family saloon, estate car and van, you could just sense there was something the brochure writer wasn't telling us. Indeed, why did one of the pictures show delivery men loading boxes through the front passenger door?

Closer inspection revealed the truth: although the Zeta looked for all the world like a wagon (a remarkably ugly one at that), some bizarre financial or engineering considerations had precluded Lightburn from providing a rear door. To gain access to the cargo area of this ghastly little box of bolts, you had to remove the seats.

There are many marks of outstanding failure and they include, but are not limited to: catastrophic sales (Morris Marina), dastardly reliability (Jensen-Healey), bombastic styling (Hyundai SLV), terrifying flimsiness (Cony Guppy), uncalled-for longevity (the Fullbore Mark X) and all of the above (Trabant P601). The 'build it and they shall come' mindset is typified by the Triumph Mayflower (they didn't come); being left alone at the outermost end of a styling trend is best shown by the doorstop-profiled, knife-edged Lagonda V8 saloon. With its 262C, Volvo took an ordinary car and turned it into something unreservedly stupid, while NSU used the Wankel-powered Ro80 to demonstrate what happens when a company confuses its ambitions with its abilities.

As for dicky science, what about the HDT Director, with its self-aligning molecules? Or the Fascination, first with its 'boilerless steam engine' then 'Electro-Magnetic Association' powerplant? This, indeed, was a case of concentrated lemon: the Fascination was ugly, daft and, finally, spectacularly unsuccessful. Not only did it have two preposterously hyped alternative energy sources, neither of them seems to have actually propelled a car under its own steam, or static electricity.

Other naff traits include unrealised promise (Rover SD1), deathly dullness (Nissan Pintara), and corporate hybrids that cleverly capture the worst aspects of two different brands. Look no further than that curious Nissan–Alfa Romeo effort called Arna, which smoothly blended Nissan flair and Alfa quality.

The Ford Pinto extended the concept of internal combustion beyond the engine, while the Quasar defied categorisation as effectively as it defied logic. The De Lorean built its lemon credentials on a solid base of hype, second-rate engineering and a consistent ability to turn out Monday morning quality at any time of any day. To these were added stunning hubris, dodgy financial dealings, lousy sales and a magnificent corporate collapse. Yes, the De Lorean was *genus motorus nafficus completus*, a car with something for every aficionado of failure.

It is worth remembering too that today's high-tech wonder car can be the latest and greatest only for a fleeting moment. Someone will always come along with something faster, sleeker or more sophisticated. A naff motor, however, can stand out for ever.

Readers of this book will find plenty of stupid names – the Daihatsu Naked and Nissan Cedric immediately spring to mind – plus two badges that have achieved the highest low accolade: they have themselves become a byword for getting it wrong. Drive forward, Ford Edsel and Austin Allegro.

There are those who defend both cars. Edsel clubs are now found across the US, despite (or more likely, because of) this model's unutterable ugliness. The heroically daft Allegro is becoming close to a 1970s retro-chic icon; the eight-track cartridge or platform shoe of cars. For all their considerable flaws, the Edsel and Allegro – and indeed the Corvair, Tucker, P76, Scamp, Zeta and Moller Skycar – are truly heroic failures, products of companies that were prepared to go out and have a red-hot go at changing the rules. Cars that are just dull, or not very good, can never really compete.

Which brings me to one last point: one man's lemon is another man's peach. Some readers will dispute my inclusions, others will decry my omissions. But enough of all that – now it's time to hit the track.

Gentlemen, start your engines. Okay, try again. Is the battery charged? Maybe it's flooded. What was that crunching noise?

Tony Davis
June 2006

1 Ford Edsel

Failure by Another Name

When Ford set up a completely new division in 1955, a snappy name was needed. Extensive surveys were undertaken and over 20,000 names considered. Learned panels debated designations including Resilient Bullet and Varsity Stroke, while market research companies studied public reaction to such extravagant monikers as Andante con Moto and Utopian Turtletop.

Having commissioned all this ground-breaking polling, Ford executives ignored it, deciding instead to use the name of the late son of the equally late Henry Ford I. Unfortunately, his name was Edsel.

Edsel was a quiet and sometimes brilliant man whom Henry had bullied, humiliated, and – some Ford family members thought – hurried to an early grave. If his name had positive connotations in Detroit, it did little to inspire the rest of the USA.

The Edsel's stylist, Roy Brown, was determined to give the new model a bold, upright grille instead of Detroit's usual horizontal treatment. His early clay models were quite stylish (in a 1950s context), but by the time every Ford executive demanded a change here or there, and every accountant found another place to trim a few cents, the eventual result was anything but.

Ridiculously overhyped throughout its development period ('the first truly new car from a Detroit manufacturer in 20 years'), the Edsel turned out to be little more than a hybrid of existing Ford and Mercury models, with new styling and a few extra gimmicks, such as a steering wheel-mounted push-button automatic gear selector and a speedometer that flashed when a preset speed was reached. The grille inset was popularly described as a 'horse collar', but Ford

people preferred the term 'impact ring'. They claimed the central bump in the hood directly above it was a safety feature, giving owners 'a sense of direction'.

In August 1957 the Edsel was unveiled to an estimated 53 million Americans during a Bing Crosby–Frank Sinatra live TV spectacular. Four versions were available – the Ranger, Corsair, Pacer, and Citation – with a choice of two huge V8s: a 361 and a 410. Named after their capacities in cubic inches, these engines were 5.9 and 6.7 litres respectively. If the Ford-generated hype on TV, in the print media, and outside every dealership across the United States wasn't enough, there was also a song:

> We want our friends to understand
> When they observe our car
> That we're as smart and successful and grand
> As we like to think we are.

The combination of the newcomer's familiar body and shockingly unfamiliar grille left one commentator to describe the Edsel as 'a Mercury pushing a toilet seat'. Even more memorable was *Time* magazine's description: 'an Oldsmobile sucking a lemon'. Despite these comments, most of the initial media was positive (further proof that, like successes, failures become more glorious with time). *Popular Science*, for example, declared, 'The Edsel – to use a horse-breeding term – is by Jaguar out of Alfa Romeo.'

Popular Science also gushed about 'more engine power than the average motorist will know what to do with, gadgets beyond a gadgeteer's dreams of glory', plus 'styling that reverses the years-long trend to horizontal-pattern front ends, and chrome enough to tax the output of the world's mines'.

However, the projected sales of 200,000 vehicles per year proved optimistic by a factor of more than three (the actual total for year one was a dismal 63,110). In 1959, when the grille was redesigned to look like a plain old horizontal Detroit job, the sales reached just 45,000, and Henry Ford II announced the whole division was for the (resilient) bullet. By then Ford had released its new Falcon, a more compact car that was on its way to setting new sales records.

The Edsel had lasted just two years and two months, and some estimates suggest Ford tore up US$250 million. The frontal styling was certainly one problem, the dismal build quality another. Equally important, the car was too expensive, a problem compounded by an economic slump. Buyers were looking for smaller, cheaper cars such as the VW Beetle, the very trend that led Detroit to develop vehicles such as the Falcon and Corvair.

By the 1960s 'edsel' had become a popular byword for lemon. The *Webster's Unabridged Dictionary* made it official.

2 Amphicar

Sea Dog

This product of German and British engineering cleverly combined the drawbacks of a car with the drawbacks of a boat.

Launched – literally – during the late 1950s, the Amphicar was one of the most successful amphibian road cars ever made, which is a very generous way of saying a few were sold before the company went broke.

The Amphicar used Triumph Herald mechanical components, an adventurous starting point considering these same components

struggled in the comparatively lightweight Herald. And the Amphicar's road manners were everything you'd expect of a heavy vehicle with a high centre of gravity that combined the wheelbase of a Mini Minor with the overall length of a family saloon.

The four-seater convertible was driven by its rear wheels on land and by twin propellers in the water. That water needed to be very still for the Amphicar to reach the claimed top water speed of 8 km/h (5 mph). In rough water it could go backwards. And there was no rudder – the front wheels were meant to make it change direction, something they didn't always want to do.

Another problem was complying with conflicting marine and road legislation: the company was dangerously close to having a vehicle that could only be used in international waters. And it was a very brave person who was prepared to lose sight of land in an Amphicar. In 1968 the whole project sank.

3 Lightburn Zeta

Fifteen Minutes of Shame

'It's a family sedan! It's a station wagon! It's a delivery wagon.' So blared the advertisements in 1963 for 'a new conception in motoring', a vehicle its manufacturers heralded as 'the culmination of ten years of research and more than one million miles of road testing'. Called Zeta, it was made 'for the world' by South Australia's Lightburn Industries, better known for its washing machines, concrete mixers, wheelbarrows, and car jacks.

This 'new conception in motoring' looked suspiciously like a big box on tiny wheels and had the sort of bug eyes you'd find in a dark corner of the fish market. What's more, the roofline clearly reflected the washing machine lineage and the nose was ugly enough to scare a gargoyle.

But if one look at the Zeta doesn't tell you why it was a showroom wallflower, consider its practical attributes. For one thing, you had to stop the engine and restart it to engage reverse. And the body, although wagon-shaped, had no rear door or hatch. You had to get the passengers out and remove the seats to load it.

If the air-duct on the bonnet suggested speed and power, this was entirely accidental. Forward motion was unwillingly provided by a Villiers two-stroke twin with a capacity of less than a third of a litre. The output was in the region of 12 kW (16 bhp), and this found its way to the front wheels via a motorcycle transmission and chain. *Wheels* magazine said of the Zeta, 'Its performance is virtually nil.'

To drive backwards, you turned the engine off and engaged an 'Electramatic' system that spun the restarted motor in the opposite direction. This gave you a full set of reverse gears and, in theory, the same top speed in either direction.

The Zeta's body was fibreglass and sat on a steel chassis. The interior was large but unremittingly sparse. The 'monkey-up-the-stick' column gearshift was a shocker, the engine a nightmare of noise, vibration, harshness, and smoke. Tackling any reasonable sized hill required a run-up of biblical proportions. And roadholding? Not very much of it at all. The fact the seats came out was advertised as a practical virtue ('ideal for watching sporting events') but was really a necessity to access the cargo area. And on and on the list went.

The head of Lightburn Industries, Harold Lightburn, assured the press that the Zeta had been designed 'not only for Australian sales but for an intensive drive on export markets'. In, say 1958, the case for the Zeta would have been a tiny bit easier to support. But from 1959,

the Mini Minor had changed everyone's ideas about how good a small car could be. Another telling fact: the Zeta cost £595 in Australia, but a Mini, complete with a boot lid and conventional reverse gear, cost only £158 more. It was no contest.

Lightburn ceased car production in 1965, having produced just 343 Zetas. That was a long way short of the 50 a week predicted, but 343 more than the company deserved.

Mercifully few, if any, made it into the wider world at the time, though a handful have left Australia in recent years for museums in the United States and Britain.

4 Mitsuoka Viewt

Tail of the Unexpected

It started in 1981 with the Zero-Honker-Bubu-Shuttle. Several major Bubus followed: the Bubu Classic SSK, the Bubu 356 Speed and the Bubu Dora. As time passed, things didn't become any less strange at the Mitsuoka car company. It continued to carve an odd niche, modifying Japanese cars to make them pale but expensive imitations of vehicles that people had stopped buying for very good reasons.

Products included a faux MG Saloon, a fake Daimler limousine and a farcical two-door convertible version of the Mark II Jaguar, each based on a different bread-and-butter Japanese model. The best-known Mitsuoka, the Coventry cat-inspired Viewt, broke cover in 1993, and 1,000 were sold in Japan over the next year, setting a Mitsuoka record.

The Viewt was based on a Nissan Micra, and its stablemate, the Galue Limousine, on the Daihatsu Applause. The K-2 was based on the incredible notion that people would want to drive a modern replica of a Messerschmitt bubble car in Tokyo traffic. The K-2 weighed 170 kg or 374 pounds (compared with, say, the sumo wrestler Konishiki, at 266 kg [586 pounds]). It was just 975 mm (38 inches) tall and was powered, if that's the word, by a 50-cc two-stroke engine.

And if Mitsuoka cars are a little odd, the company's sales literature is even more so. 'Become acquainted with the Viewt', one brochure

declares, 'and you'll become so involved, it will make your lover
jealous.' The same brochure says the Galue takes its inspiration from
'a particular sort of individual . . . one who is not selfish, but like a
stubborn father of old with rigid bones, possesses an underlying
kindness'. It has 'a front grille that other cars cannot compete with . . .
will not be affected by changing fashions and can be long-loved'.

5 De Lorean DMC-12

Back to the Maker

John Zachary De Lorean was a gifted engineer and, by all reports, a real charmer. The bejewelled playboy certainly impressed General Motors, which made him head of its Pontiac division. Then 'GM's youngest-ever vice president' leapt even higher. He became boss of Chevrolet and convinced almost everyone within earshot that GM's lavish presidential office was his for the taking. It was not to be. By 1973 De Lorean was dogged by whispers of financial impropriety and resigned, mumbling something about 'pursuing a dream'.

John Z assisted with a bitter book called *On a Clear Day (You Can See General Motors)* and set up his own company to build 'an ethical car'. Unlike most dreamers, De Lorean eventually got his automobile company up and running. Unfortunately, however, the ethics his car reflected were his own, rather than those of the broader community.

To get the project off the ground, De Lorean had to first convince a few important people their money was safest in his care. The socialist British government of James Callaghan was as unlikely a source of cash as any. Next thing, our man was sitting on £55 million of British taxpayers' money on the condition he made his US-bound cars in the very troubled Northern Ireland.

Soon a plant popped up in Dunmurry (near Belfast) and John Z attempted to show 2,500 inexperienced workers how to turn out

gullwing-doored, stainless-steel-bodied, rear-engined V6 sports cars from scratch at a proposed rate of 20,000 per annum. That the fine folk of Dunmurry weren't very successful at this wasn't really their fault. The design, penned years earlier by Giorgio Giugiaro, was under-developed, with production schedules founded on blue-sky optimism.

Lotus's founder, Colin Chapman, was brought in to solve the manifest problems, but he proved far more interested in helping John Z pocket the British government loans, grants, and special subsidies than in straightening out the production line. When the piggy bank was empty, De Lorean threatened to close the plant and push the workers back on to the street unless the government, now run by Margaret Thatcher, gave him another £30 million. It did.

The De Lorean DMC-12 was finally released in mid-1981, and the build quality was woeful. Furthermore, the DMC-12 was tail-heavy and noisy and slow and expensive to build. Visibility was poor, the stainless-steel bodywork was fragile and in no sense stainless, while the electrically powered gullwing doors were outrageously heavy, glacial in their movement and prone to leaking. When the electrics failed (no rare thing) the occupants were forced to climb out through the rear hatch.

Sales were calamitous. Those customers who had been found wanted their money back, and within a year the De Lorean Motor Company was put in the hands of a bankruptcy administrator. By then it was discovered that about £10 million of research money had been diverted to dodgy bank accounts in Switzerland and Panama.

In October 1982 the British administrator announced the final failure of rescue attempts. Within hours John Z was arrested for trafficking US$24 million worth of cocaine, an indiscretion allegedly undertaken to raise money to keep the company afloat. Meanwhile, as the legal net closed tighter, Colin Chapman succumbed to a fatal heart attack (or disappeared, if you believe the most outlandish of the conspiracy theories). De Lorean managed to beat the drug charges but the defence was entrapment. Rather than, for example, 'I didn't do it.'

Around 8,500 De Loreans were made (records are contradictory). In the mid-1980s the film *Back to the Future* made the DMC-12 famous for the second time. The film made money.

John De Lorean died in March 2005. By that time he was penniless and living mainly on social security. Many of the people he had done business with were in a similar situation.

6 Hyundai SLV

Ducking for Cover

From the moment it was unveiled at the 1997 Seoul Motor Show, Hyundai's SLV concept car divided observers. There were those who didn't like it, and those who absolutely despised it.

Nobody, however, failed to notice the Korean 'Super Luxury Vehicle', with its Picasso-with-a-hangover styling and monstrous exterior dimensions (5.6 metres or 18.5 feet long and roughly halfway

between 'too wide' and 'much too wide'). Hyundai's official line was that the SLV's fibre-reinforced polymer body was 'eye-catching', but an executive from a rival brand, Daewoo, got a lot more mileage with the line, 'It looks like the car Scrooge McDuck uses to take his money to the bank.'

The car was so unpopular with motor show crowds that its builder avoided the usual tease line of 'this concept car is a good indication of the styling of our exciting new models to come'. Instead, Hyundai's supremo, Mr B.J. Park, carefully explained to anyone who would listen that the company had 'no intention of developing a production model that looks anything like the SLV'.

7 Triumph Stag

A Lavish Flaw Show

When an owner stands by his Triumph Stag, it's usually because he can't get the door open. Yet there was a time when the Stag seemed to represent an exciting future for sports cars. The styling was well received, the technical specifications (including independent rear suspension) and luxury features also impressed, while the two-plus-two seating lent a degree of practicality not usually found in open sports cars.

Most impressively, the clever T-bar roof circumvented 1970s safety legislation that appeared destined to outlaw convertibles. But in the end, the convertible luxury Triumph was famous mainly for being famously unreliable, and its optimistic early buyers were soon thoroughly Stagmatised.

The newcomer was based on a svelte 1965 show car by Michelotti, but Triumph – by now a division of British Leyland – was somehow deluded into thinking a stylish body could lift its image and allow it to compete with Mercedes and the like. If delusions of grandeur were not enough, the Stag was engineered in a hurry, built on a shoestring, put together with nothing even approaching care, and backed by an imploding Leyland.

Launched in the UK in July 1970 to a good media response and a strong order bank, the Stag soon became just another Leyland horror

story. It cost the company millions in warranty claims, and millions more were spent in the frantic but ultimately unsuccessful attempt to fix the inherent design problems as production continued.

For a mystifying reason, the engineers had decided against using the lightweight alloy-block Rover V8 engine, which in various forms would power a wide range of British Leyland vehicles, including the Range Rover and P76. They may have decided it wasn't unreliable enough to wear Triumph nameplates; either way, they opted to join two Triumph Dolomite four-cylinder engines via a common crankshaft to create a unique, and uniquely horrible, 3-litre V8. Chronic overheating often led to major engine damage. If that didn't get you, timing-chain failure would. Or the crankshaft bearings, or . . . you get the picture. And for all that, the home-made V8 produced only 109 kW (145 bhp), leaving the long, narrow, and fairly heavy 1,275 kg (3,170 pounds) Stag chronically short of breath.

The Stag's price was daftly high at the start and nearly doubled within a few years. Still, by 1975 there were 16,500 examples on UK roads. Or pulled over at the side with the bonnet up. About 7,700 had been exported by that time, too. Most of the exports went to the US where the car was launched in 1971 and discontinued by popular demand just seventeen months later.

Standard equipment ran to electric windows, power steering, and wood-grained dash. Although the Stag had four seats, the rear was a kids-only zone, and the downside of the clever T-bar construction was high wind noise. Amazingly, this became even louder when the optional hardtop was fitted. This ludicrously heavy removable roof was best installed with the help of a football team, yet it invariably leaked.

The Stag Mark II of 1973 brought a blacked-out tail panel and blacked-out door sills, which wasn't exactly addressing the sharp end of the problem. Despite its reputation, the Stag staggered on until June 1977. In his book *Making Money from Collectable Cars* (Marque Publishing 1988), Cliff Chambers put it very succinctly: 'As an investment, the Stag is best ignored, since maintenance costs will exceed any profits you may make. But if you are a mechanical masochist, this is your car.'

8 Daihatsu Naked

Comic Strip

In 1998 Daihatsu decided there was a niche for a car aimed at buyers who wanted the Schwarzenegger-tough look of an American military Hummer, but were actually hobbits.

The slab-sided automotive midget that resulted was called the Naked. Yes, you heard correctly: Naked. Why? Perhaps somebody had already registered the name Stupid.

Forward motion came from a 660-cc (40-cubic-inch) twin-turbo engine, while other features included a 'relocatable instrument panel' and 'detachable multi-air folding rear seats'. No, we don't have a clue either. Maybe we should check with someone who is less than three feet tall and has hairy feet . . .

According to the Japanese marketing guff, the Naked was 'so basic, it's advanced', and the company president Iichi Shingu described it as a vehicle 'that could only have been created by Daihatsu'. This comment met with little disagreement.

9 Lagonda V8 Saloon

Shock Wedge

There are few brands with a history as chequered as Lagonda, founded in Britain in 1906 by a sewing-machine engineer from Ohio. And few brands of any origin have built anything as outrageous as the Lagonda V8 Saloon.

The compressed background is this: Lagonda won the 1935 Le Mans 24-Hour race while the company staved off financial ruin for the umpteenth time. In 1947, after a few more close encounters with the official bankruptcy administrator, the company was purchased by the David Brown tractor group (which already owned Aston Martin, another brand no stranger to financial problems). Lagonda cars ceased production in the early 1960s, but the brand was reactivated in 1976 for this, the V8 Saloon.

The styling was the work of William Towns, the man responsible for various Aston Martin models, including the DB-S coupé. The Lagonda V8's steel body, its wedge shape reminiscent of a door stop, was dropped on to the extended chassis of an Aston Martin two-door. The 5.3-litre V8 engine, for the most part hand-built, produced in the region of 250 kW (333 bhp), thanks to four twin-throated Webers, and squished out its power through a Chrysler Torqueflite automatic transmission. To this point it all sounds like fairly normal Aston Martin fare, an impression reinforced by the presence of lots of dead cow and polished tree in the interior. But take a deep breath . . .

The *Star Trek*-like interior was intended to be as futuristic as the exterior. Unfortunately it was. There was an over-the-top single-spoke steering wheel, soft-touch switches and an LED digital instrument panel that, with the common sense of hindsight, looks like the display from one of those build-it-yourself digital watches sold by electronic stores of that era (though was less reliable).

For a brief period the reborn Lagonda was heralded as 'the world's most expensive saloon'. It was certainly a more accurate tag than 'the world's best'. More than anything, the Lagonda V8 Saloon represented a bargain-basement attempt to use existing mechanical components in a body envelope that afforded almost no room for such things as engine ancillaries and exhaust plumbing. All the bits (most borrowed from the high-bonneted Aston models) needed to be shoehorned, rerouted, and generally crammed under that daftly flat and low nose. Reliability problems were legion.

Autocar magazine called it 'the world's only four-door two-plus-two', a reference to the almost complete lack of space afforded the rear passengers. Lagonda's wedge was also a shocker to park, on account of the long, low snout. And it was not much more fun to drive quickly, courtesy of overly soft suspension. Performance was more leisurely than power figures might suggest, though this was a luxury saloon, the makers reminded us, not a sports coupé. If speed was the primary consideration, an Aston Martin coupé or convertible was available.

Rarely has a piece of futuristic design dated so quickly. Yet ironically, the wedge sold better than its Aston coupé cousins produced at the same Newport Pagnell headquarters, thanks to it being a favourite of sorts in the Middle East.

The Lagonda V8 Saloon had been launched at £25,000; a decade later the ask was an almost unbelievable £75,000. Amazingly, it stumbled on until 1990. By then the overly square design cues had been rounded, the interior had been redone, and the mechanical bugs, if not completely squashed, had certainly received a good whack on the head with a shoe. The suspension had also been tweaked and the car was at last heralded as a good thing to drive. But the best thing about driving it remained the fact that you couldn't see it from behind the wheel.

More than 600 examples of the V8 Saloon were eventually produced. However, the Aston Martin–Lagonda outfit continued to be a serial offender when it came to going broke, being bought out and going broke again. It was finally put out of its misery when Ford grabbed it in 1987, becoming the sixth owner in fifteen years.

10 Ford Nucleon

Atomic Bomb

It was in 1958 that Ford unveiled a car that took advantage of the latest, greatest alternative fuel source: nuclear power. The Nucleon, displayed at American motor shows as a scale model rather than a full-size 'concept', was claimed to be capable of travelling 4,800 miles (7,680 km) without refuelling.

The strange placement of the wheels was said to be due to the huge weight of the reactor. One could expect that after more than a few minutes in the cantilevered front seat, the Nucleon owner would get seasickness – and perhaps a migraine in the second head growing out of the middle of his chest. Sample morning radio traffic report: 'The state of California was evacuated this morning after a two-Nucleon collision.'

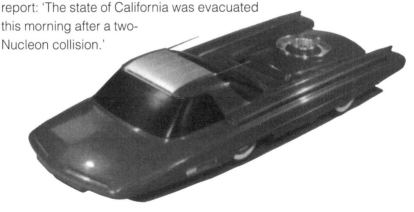

11 Suzuki X90

Coming, Ready or Not

'You've never driven anything like this before!' announced the Suzuki X90 brochure, and for once a brochure was accurate. The conveyance in question was squat and unsightly, daft in concept and lousy in packaging. And it rode like a boneshaker bicycle. The X90 was originally shown in concept form at the Tokyo Motor Show, supposedly to test public reaction. The public reacted, but Suzuki proceeded anyway.

At the heart of the X90's genesis seems to be the belief that although the US was going mad for big trucks and Suzuki only built small ones, the Americans just might embrace something at Suzuki's end of the scale if it were different enough. And the X90 was certainly that.

Just to be sure, Suzuki decided to build it in right-hand drive as well for the Japanese, British and Australian markets. The first production X90s hit showrooms in 1996 and its maker boasted the newcomer represented a 'triumph in pure visual appeal'. A vehicle responsible for such a remarkable accomplishment in aesthetics might have been expected to command a large premium in the market. However, Suzuki had cold feet from the start and the X90 started out at a relatively modest price.

In the UK the base model was not hugely dearer than Suzuki's bare-bones Vitara soft-top, despite having a T-Top targa roof and a great deal more standard equipment. It still refused to move and it

soon became obvious that salespeople would have had an easier time clearing diplodocus evacuations from their showroom floors.

The mechanical components were for the most part borrowed from the Vitara, with a 1.6-litre four-cylinder engine and rear-wheel drive in the cheapest version in most markets. A dual ratio 4WD set-up was also available, either on the tiny chance that a buyer would take an X90 off the road, or in the belief that potential buyers could be suckered into thinking it would make the X90's handling less evil on the road. Needless, to say it didn't.

The brochure boasted of such safety features as 'three-point seatbelts, side impact protection, head restraints', all of which were the bare minimum required by law. However, in some markets (including the UK) Suzuki threw in an airbag or two.

'In the Xtreme' was the slogan, a reference perhaps to a body with the packaging efficiency of a roadster, whacked on top of a drivetrain that ensured the high centre of gravity, rotten dynamics, uncomfortable ride and questionable on-road safety of an all-terrain vehicle (although the word 'coupé' was often used about the 'is it coming or going?' two-door bodywork, no reviewer ever used the phrase 'coupé-like handling'). Another problem was the vehicle's strictly two-seater nature, coupled with a small boot further cramped by a poorly placed spare wheel and bulky pockets for housing the T-Top roof panels.

Production of the X90 spluttered to a halt in 1998, but it was well into 1999 that the last examples were inflicted on customers. Suzuki muttered something about the concept being ahead of its time. Yeah, right.

12 Fullbore Mark X

Everything Old is Old Again

Look familiar? Contempt-breedingly so? Perhaps that's because the Fullbore Mark X of the 1990s was merely an updated and re-Anglicised version of the Hindustan Ambassador, a model that had been built in Calcutta since 1959 and was itself based on the Morris Oxford.

By the time it was again sold in England, the Morris/Hindustan/ Fullbore was fitted with an Indian-assembled 1.8-litre Isuzu engine, plus such delights as drum brakes all round (with no power assistance) and what was described as Foot-o-Matic windscreen wipers. What the 'matic' bit referred to is unclear – you cleared the screen with a very manual thump of your left foot.

The London-based importing company Fullbore Motors promoted the Mark X as a robust, no-nonsense car that one could comfortably drive while wearing a hat . 'The Fullbore Mark X is a fine compromise between the charm of the 1950s and the mechanical strength and build quality of the 1990s,' said a spokesman, perhaps getting it the wrong way around.

To give at least a hint of the second decade referred to in this rather optimistic assessment, the car was repainted and retrimmed when it hit the Southampton docks. There, such niceties as seatbelts, mirrors, a catalytic converter, and chrome hubcaps were added, and all liquid was drained from the cooling system and washer bottles for fear of bringing in water-borne diseases. Despite all this effort, the Fullbore company seems to have fallen off the map around 1998.

13 Jaguar XJS

Sour Puss

Beware any vehicle that people defend with the phrase: 'Yes, but it has lots of character.' When those fateful words are uttered you know it's a Jaguar or an Alfa Romeo that is being discussed and some poor owner is throwing buckets of money into a black hole with the misguided notion that he or she is taking part in a 'special experience'.

Look no further than the Jaguar XJS coupé. If an elephant is a greyhound designed by a committee, then an XJS is, similarly, a sports car suffering from far too much conciliation and arbitration. In an attempt to upset no one, and in effect pleasing exactly the same number of people, Jaguar ignored the golden rule of sports-car building: it has to come from the heart.

The looks weren't the worst thing about this mid-1970s indiscretion. With the XJS, Jaguar almost perfectly combined the comfort of a sports car with the agility of a limousine.

The XJS was impressive in a straight line, certainly, but only when the insanely complicated, notoriously thirsty V12 engine was working. Jaguars of the mid-1970s to mid-1980s were so unreliable that many Jaguar dealers made 80 per cent of their profits out the back door. Which is a way of saying that four out of every five dollars coming into the dealership were for spare parts and repairs.

The starting point for the XJS was the legendary E-Type Jaguar. This had been launched in 1961 to rave reviews and, even if it had become fat and outdated in its lifetime, it remained a more interesting car than its replacement. And what wasn't known at the time of the changeover was that cost pressures would mean that the XJS would need to stay on sale for twenty years, forcing Jaguar to enter the multimedia age with the automotive equivalent of a valve radio.

This writer dug up some notes from the last new XJS he drove, circa 1992: 'seat doesn't go far enough back, no room next to the brake pedal, forced to curl left foot around the brake pedal . . . sore after twenty minutes of driving. Excessive wind-noise at 60 km/h [about 35 mph, and this was the steel-roofed version!]. Bodywork covered in ill-fitting, overlapping chrome mouldings. Steers like a speedboat; weighs a massive 1,860 kg (4,100 pounds) and feels it. Carpet slid away underfoot, to reveal a mess of wires, rough felt and assorted plastic pieces.'

The list went on. And so did the XJS, not getting a well-warranted bullet behind the left ear until 1996.

14 Riley Elf

Minor Catastrophe

After the Second World War, the British Motor Corporation (BMC) enjoyed a 46 per cent share of the British car market and controlled many of the most revered automotive brand names in the history of the Sceptred Isle. Yet it managed to squander both its market share and every single one of the brand values of every single one of those brands. Evidence of how it accomplished this feat is provided by such ludicrous conveyances as the Riley Elf.

No points for guessing that this 1961 atrocity was an adaptation of the Mini Minor, cleverly preserving the cramped interior without maintaining the compact, park-anywhere exterior dimensions. And, in the process, turning the simple and elegant into the ornate and ugly. If the Riley Elf wasn't silly enough, there was a Wolseley Hornet version, too.

15 Morris Marina

To Err Is Leyland

The Marina provided a textbook example of how not to design a car, engineer a car, build a car or sell a car.

It came about because the newly formed British Leyland Motor Corporation decided it needed a competitor for the highly successful Ford Escort. The rather desperate starting point was a slightly stretched version of the Morris Minor platform but, during the shambolic development programme that followed, the car grew bigger, heavier and more expensive.

'We meant to do that,' muttered various executives. But deep down they realised they had inadvertently produced a competitor not for the Escort but for the bigger Ford Cortina. Worse still, they had ended up with a car that was more expensive to build than the Cortina, despite the engines and almost everything else being borrowed from the Leyland parts bin. A vast, last-minute cost-cutting campaign was mounted ahead of the 1971 launch, and this helped strip the forthcoming vehicle of any charm, solidity or reliability that it might have otherwise had. But it still didn't make it profitable.

And so it was that the poorly conceived, stupidly named, excruciatingly dull, financially ruinous, badly built box of bolts called Marina went on sale in 1971. Most four-cylinder Leyland cars of the era were front-drive but the Marina powered its rear wheels. This was

in keeping with the objective of producing a simple and rugged car that would overcome the reliability problems for which the organisation had become a byword. Management was also convinced the rear-drive configuration would give the new model appeal to the fleet customers who were lapping up Escorts and Cortinas instead of front-drive Austins.

On launch day there were 1.3- and 1.8-litre four-cylinder engines on offer and an exterior colour selection that comprised the dullest hues of beige and brown and the occasional misguided dalliance with metallic purple and 'limeflower green'. The range of body styles grew to include saloon, coupé and wagon plus a couple of commercial variants, yet fleet customers remained as uninterested as private buyers. Even aged care organisations and councils thought it was too dull.

Furthermore, although the Marina was simple, it wasn't rugged. It seemed to have been built by people who had more important or more interesting things to do.

The driving experience was crude at best, the handling was on the unfashionable side of ordinary, mechanical noise was excruciating and almost everything else about the Marina felt old-fashioned even on day one. The suspension was shocking in a literal sense. This not only gave the occupants a jarring time, it hurried along all those badly attached parts that were already thinking of leaving. Compare Marina with what Ford of Europe, Volkswagen and the better Japanese companies were doing at that time and it isn't hard to see the size of the problem.

To match its nautical nomenclature, the newcomer had a tendency to fill with water at the slightest hint of rain. The performance also suggested that the Marina had a few too many boats moored to it. Indeed, it was such a bad car it is hard to believe that anybody could have made it worse. However, in late 1973 Leyland Australia engineers met that challenge. They squeezed the P76's 2.6-litre six-cylinder engine under the bonnet, turning an underpowered pig into an understeering pig with hideously heavy controls and handling that occupied that slender niche between very bad and bloody awful. (The Marina wasn't the only English car Downunder that copped a crude six under the bonnet. Around the same time Ford Australia added a six-cylinder engine to the locally produced Cortina, transforming a nimble medium-sized saloon into a nose-heavy, fuel-gulping horror.)

On the home-front, the Marina was forced to stumble on through strikes, power cuts, restructures and a government bail-out. And changing the name didn't make a bad car better or more popular; an attempt to sell the car in Canada with an Austin badge was another monumental flop.

In 1980 the Marina's nose and tail were reworked in an attempt to hide the ancient underpinnings. Because this bargain basement restyle was completed with a little technical help from Giorgetto Giugiaro's famous ItalDesign studio, Leyland renamed the car the Morris Ital in the hope of convincing people it was possessed of some sort of Italian design magic. It wasn't.

The Ital lasted until the launch of the Austin Montego in 1984, at which point the Morris name was finally put out to pasture.

16 Volvo 262C

Anyone for Squash?

Throughout the 1970s Volvo was flying a holding pattern. It developed its box-on-a-box 140 series into the equally boxy 240 series and then killed off its weird-as-all-get-up but fondly remembered P1800 coupé (as driven by Roger Moore in the original British television series of *The Saint*).

The company's image was slipping in every market, while economic factors were making the once-affordable 'Swedish taxis' far too expensive. Against this background, the company's president, P.G. Gyllenhammer, commanded his designers to produce something really special, something that would revitalise Volvo's luxury image and create unprecedented excitement for the brand. Gyllenhammer, a genuinely messianic speaker, no doubt delivered this request in something akin to a Swedish rendition of the hugely stirring St Crispin's Day speech in Shakespeare's *Henry V*. And spurred on by this rousing, poetic call to arms, what did Volvo's finest produce? The 262C.

The Volvo 262C, first sold in 1977, was just about the dumbest coupé derivative ever built. Even though it had entirely new bodywork turned out at vast expense by the Italian autobody builder and design house Bertone, it looked for all the world like an everyday Volvo saloon that had been hit by a lift.

The daftly low roofline that defined the car was not a clever optical illusion. It was achieved entirely at the expense of headroom. About 2.5 inches disappeared, along with a great deal of rear visibility, making a mockery of Volvo's constant crowing about putting safety first.

In the US magazine *Car and Driver*, journalist Rich Ceppos pointed out that at US$16,000, the 262C cost two grand more than a Cadillac Eldorado. 'If you're a normal-sized adult,' he added, 'an ability to magically shrink your torso is what's needed to fit inside without hitting your head.'

The English motoring press scratched its collective head at the term 'limited edition' – the appearance alone would have guaranteed that – and the idea that this stunted two-door could be priced at £13,000, or 50 per cent more than the range-topping saloon, the 264GLE. In Australia, where the asking price was an even more exorbitant Aus$32,000, *Wheels* magazine called it 'the car for little people with big wallets'. Rival *Motor Manual* reported that a bystander had asked its road tester, 'Who squashed ya car, mate?'

Mechanically, the newcomer was standard Volvo 260 series: rear-wheel drive, front engine. It used the shared Renault–Peugeot–Volvo 2.6-litre OHC V6, a dull-as donk [engine] that gave Volvo sixes of the day a slower 0-to-60 mph acceleration time than their cheaper four-cylinder stablemates.

The 262C's interior had all the required luxury items (lots of dead tree and cow, and plenty of electric assistance), while the bodywork carried Volvo and Bertone badges plus what looked like a funny swirly crown. This was the crest of the king of Sweden, who apparently was a great fan of the design. And evidently no basketball champion.

There were various theories about the reasons for the 262C's dubious styling. The most convincing was that the designers at Volvo didn't have a bloody clue. Consider the statement made at the time of the car's launch by Volvo's chief designer, Jan Wilksgaard: 'The 262C brings out the underlying sporty elegance that Volvo has always perceived as their image and expresses it more clearly. It's a very personal car that makes a statement.'

Buyers made their own statement: 'You must be joking.'

17 Arbib Dome Car

Bubble Rap

Styled by the industrial designer and artist Richard Arbib, and built circa 1961 by Andrew Mazzeri, a New York 'autobody builder', the Arbib Dome Car was presumably thought to be beautiful. And who are we to say otherwise? Ugly bugger, isn't it?

Powered by a four-cylinder engine and largely made of aluminium, the Arbib used an electric motor to raise and lower its glass dome. This prototype was said to have cost the then-massive sum of US$35,000. But, for reasons that totally mystify, series production did not follow.

18 Mini Moke

Dare to be Bare

Like some missing link between the vintage and modern automobile (or the skateboard and soapbox racer, if you want to be particularly cruel) is the box-sided, doorless, windowless Mini Moke. The Moke story – the name came from a slang word for donkey or inferior horse – started in the late 1950s, when the British Motor Corporation (BMC) answered the call for a light vehicle for the UK army.

Unfortunately, BMC's answer wasn't the one the military was looking for. The boys in green rather selfishly demanded good ground clearance, easy maintenance, and go-anywhere performance. The Moke couldn't offer the first, with its tiny 25.4-cm (10-inch) wheels, fell down on the second count, with its complex Mini Minor power train, and failed on the third due to front-wheel drive. In an attempt to give the vehicle some measure of Jeep capability while preserving the compact size (after all, the Moke was designed to be stacked flat in aircraft cargo holds), some experimental four-wheel-drive versions were built. One had an engine and transmission at each end, like a bodiless, push-me-pull-you Mini.

By 1963 the army had rejected every variation BMC could come up with, so it was decided to make a civilian version. This went on sale in 1964 with two-wheel drive and (just one) 850-cc engine. It was motoring at its most basic, with a punt-style chassis made from steel

pressings, and pannier-style boxes along each side to give rigidity and house the battery, fuel tank, and tool kit. Not surprisingly, the lack of bodywork proved a problem in Old Blighty weather and buyers stayed away in record numbers. It was then that BMC, in accordance with English tradition, sent the unwanted to the colonies.

Moke production was transferred to Australia in 1966, where the vehicle quickly became known as the Mini Joke. In standard form, only two seats were fitted and there was no rollover protection.

Weather protection, meanwhile, amounted to a fold-away (and often blow-away) fabric roof. As well as being cold and wet for much of the year, Moke drivers had to endure Mini-Minor reliability without even getting Mini weather protection or a lockable boot.

At least the Moke was cheap, for much of its life bearing the mantle of the least expensive four-wheeled road vehicle on the Australian market. Out in the bush, the Moke was expected to find a ready market among farmers who couldn't afford Land Rovers. The hitch proved to be the relative lack of power and the low ground clearance, which combined to make it an almost useless workhorse. In 1968, BMC Australia offered optional 33-cm (13-inch) wheels, a year later a 1.1-litre engine was fitted. This turned the Moke's fortunes around, er, 360 degrees.

The Moke's failure as a working vehicle led to a refocusing of its image as a fun recreational vehicle ('Things go better with Moke',

cried one ad) and, alternatively, the ultimate thrift machine ('Moking is not a wealth hazard', cried another). By the early 1970s a new version known as the Californian was on sale, complete with paisley vinyl soft-top, lurid body colours, improved seats and a 1,275-cc (77.5-cubic-inch) engine. Further upgrades were made through the 1970s.

In 1976 a Danish-born adventurer, Hans Tholstrup, used his Moke and rubber dinghy hybrid to cross the notoriously rough Bass Strait between Tasmania and the Australian mainland. Such stunts were not enough to save the Moke, though; it never achieved a 2CV-style cult following, though there are now a few clubs around the world, including in the UK and North America.

Production of Australian Mokes ceased in 1981, after a total of 26,142 had been built for local and overseas markets. That's a miserable average of 1,600 per year, but the story didn't end there. Production was again transferred, this time to Portugal, where Mokes were built until 1992. The tooling was then sold to the Italian company Cagiva, which produced a further 1,500 or so in Portugal then shipped the tooling to Italy. And there lies the Moke's main claim to fame: very few cars in history have stayed in continuous production for thirty years without ever being a success.

19 Gaia Deltoid

Echoes of Something

'Nothing like it' was the slogan for this 1996 three-wheeled British, er, vehicle. Seldom have truer words been spoken. It wasn't just the styling that seemed to have fallen out of a different time-space continuum. The full name was 'the Gaia Deltoid Supertrikar' (GDS).

The GDS consisted of a two-seater cockpit with a patent-applied-for 'headstock coupling' that allowed a wide variety of motorcycle rear ends to be bolted into the back. The bike's rear wheel was intended to provide all of the go and a third of the stop. Despite incorporating

some of the disadvantages of a motorcycle, the tape measure showed the GDS was a very car-like 4 metres (13 feet) long. It weighed not much more than 400 kg (880 pounds), however, and depending on the bike selected, was said to be quick, very quick, or 'warp drive'.

Details of exactly what happened to the GDS venture after its bold launch are hard to locate. So are examples of the Supertrikar, although I did find a brochure. It boldly states that the vehicle 'draws on the past as much as the future', and provides 'echoes of old and new Ferraris and Porsches mingled with the feeling of a racing sports car'. That is certainly one interpretation. Another is that it looks like a Mardi Gras float. Just add flight crew.

20 Alfasud

The Corrode Warrior

It was the car that gave rust a bad name. Even terms such as 'gross mechanical unreliability' were reluctant to be mentioned in the same sentence. It was the Alfasud, a mini Alfa Romeo that was in some ways the world's best small car and in others the most horrible vehicle of any size.

Some of the faults – such as a remote boot-release handle on the passenger side (only slightly closer to the driver than the boot) – were there by design. Others were specially added during the production process. Many of the things in this second category had nothing to do with carelessness. They were the result of great attention to detail. It was all to do with north–south Italian rivalry.

The background is this: Alfa Romeo traditionally built its cars in Milan, but in the 1960s the company announced a surprise plan to decentralise in a southerly direction. The new plant was to be in Naples and was to build the lower-cost Alfasud (*sud* being Italian for south) at the unprecedented rate of 1,000 cars a day. The folks in the north didn't take very well to the concept of jobs being sent south. Sabotage might be too severe a word, but the components built in Milan and sent to Naples to be fitted to Alfasuds were bad even by the standards set by Alfa Romeo's northern plant.

To add to this rather fundamental problem, the southern plant had been built in a rush (to meet a target of three years from open field to mass production) and staffed with many people who had never built cars before and didn't appear to be in a hurry to learn. The fruit of all this, er, creative tension was unveiled at the Turin Motor Show in late 1971. The 'Sud' was a small four-door sedan with attractive lines and a surprisingly affordable price tag. However, the equipment level was sparse enough to preclude carpet, a radio, and any method of propping up the boot lid (when open, it rested on the rear window). Decent ventilation was also off the list. Yet all this and more was forgiven by many road testers once they punted a Sud down a challenging piece of road.

The Alfasud was front-wheel drive, a layout not widely considered sporty. But reviewers enthusiastically (and justifiably) pointed out that the Sud set totally new standards of roadholding for a small car. The space efficiency was also excellent, and, providing you didn't mind rowing along the gear lever, the perky little 1.2-litre 'boxer' (or horizontally opposed) engine gave exhilarating performance.

However, while the ink was still drying on rave reviews, many customers were seeing their Suds spitting, clunking, and shuddering to a halt. And the biggest problem of all, rust, was yet to appear.

Early Sud glitches went beyond the rattles and squeaks considered to be part of normal Alfa 'character'. The doors quickly drooped and needed to be slammed. This in turn knocked the flimsy door-mounted side mirrors out of whack. The weather sealing was poor, which exacerbated the corrosion problem, the wind noise was high, the interior door handles fell off, and an Alfasud floor was rarely without a rich covering of small plastic bits that had come from somewhere under the dash or seats.

The high-revving nature of the engine (and, to be fair, the sort of boy racers who bought the car) had a devastating effect. Owners experienced such problems as spark-plug leads that rattled free, carburettors that choked themselves, and throttle cables that jammed. This was often in the lead-up to more extravagant failures involving enormous mechanical crunching noises and clouds of black smoke. However, rust was the fatal problem. It appeared under the engine bay of many cars within months of delivery and would eventually eat doors, sills, windscreen surrounds, and roofs. The proof is in the vanishing: large numbers of Suds were sold in many countries, but they are very thin on the ground today.

21 Lada Samara

Blunderbuss

This Eastern Bloc Shocker was launched in 1984, and was by far the most modern car to come out of Russia. Which isn't saying much, except that it never should have come out of Russia.

Originally known as the VAZ Sputnik, and offered with a 1.1-litre engine, the five-door hatch took over the production line from the boxy Lada 1500, which was based on a 1960s Fiat saloon. (The USSR was a big buyer of Fiat technology, which it paid for in second-rate steel that the Fiat Group used in Alfa Romeos. And sadly, that is *not* an urban legend.)

By 1984 standards, Russia's finest had a relatively modern mechanical configuration (well, it was front-wheel drive) and an almost stylish hatchback body. But even at twenty paces you could see the woeful nature of such things as body fit and colour matching, as well as the nastiness of the plastics used in the bumpers and grille. This writer composed a list of faults with the first example he drove, a 1.5-litre three-door from 1988, and covered two tightly packed foolscap pages. Everything that could squeak squeaked; many things that should have worked didn't. And bits of the dashboard actually fell off.

Exports sales – never strong – petered out in most places in the 1990s, though the model lingered on in its homeland until the end of the century.

22 Goggomobil Dart

Gee, Oh! Gee, Gee, Oh!

The Bruce Weiner Microcar Museum in Georgia (USA) is one of the few museums in the world to concentrate on cars at the minuscule end of the scale. Among its collection is a perfectly preserved Goggomobil Dart, which the catalogue describes as 'a pretty two seater in the then-current Lotus idiom'.

But as someone who once owned one, I won't hear a nice word said about it. My Goggo, a black Dart with a mind-shattering 12.5 kW (16.6 bhp) lighting up the back wheels (and pulsing, grabbing drum brakes lighting up the front wheels), was bought twenty-five years after the event. It was in genuine 'as-new' condition, which proved to be no benefit.

The story behind this most eccentric vehicle takes us back to the 1950s and a man named Bill Buckle, based in Sydney, Australia. Buckle had previously launched a classy and expensive coupé bearing his own name, but the Goggomobil was at the other extreme. It came after Buckle purchased the local rights to the tiny German Goggomobil with the intention of marrying imported mechanicals with fibreglass bodies produced Downunder.

The result, launched in 1958, was the smallest and cheapest 'family' car on the Aussie market. The two-seater Dart sports variant – conceived and designed by Buckle himself – followed in 1959.

The Dart was only a fraction more than a metre tall, and its other statistics were equally oddball. The weight of 340 kg (748 pounds) put it halfway between a motorcycle and a car, which made perfect sense for a vehicle that combined the disadvantages of both.

There were no doors. To help with ingress and egress, the seats rose slightly when you pulled them back. However, the climb over the sides was not dignified. And you didn't get out of the minuscule Dart so much as flick it off. The original press release said that 'safety was a number-one priority'. Yet no one in a Dart ever felt even slightly secure. While you looked up at other cars' door handles, the other road users looked straight over you. And if you needed a sudden burst of acceleration, it was best to jump out and run.

The ride was bone-shaking and the steering as light as you'd expect in a such a tiny car. The steering was also billy-cart direct: about one hiccup lock to lock. There was no luggage space and little weather protection (a fold-up roof was optional, but as the Goggomobil had no doors, when the roof was up it completely trapped the occupants inside). The four-speed motorcycle transmission had the oddest shift pattern in the automotive kingdom and every other Dart feature was on the quirky side of peculiar.

The engine was a two-stroke but felt like less. Placed in the tail, it displaced under a third of a litre (293-cc, to be exact), had a 6:1 compression ratio, and developed its maximum speed at what seemed to be about 95,000 rpm. The top speed was approximately 100 km/h (a bit over 60 mph), at which point the engine made almost enough noise to drown out the sound of pedestrians laughing as you drove past.

For all that, the Goggomobil had the distinction of being the only independently produced Australian car to make money during the 1950s. Around 5,000 cars were built (most were 'family sedan' models but the total also included 700 Darts), before the Mini Minor arrived and completely changed the economy car landscape.

23 Mitsubishi HSR-VI

Stiff Competition

Between 1987 and 1997 Mitsubishi thought it necessary to build not one, not two, but six generations of its HSR concept car. Each was just that little bit sillier than the one before, reaching a peak, so to speak, with the HSR-VI.

This was an 'automated driving mode' vehicle with clamshell doors that inexplicably opened directly into the path of anyone trying to enter or exit the vehicle.

Mitsubishi had variously used the HSR label to stand for High Speed Running, Human Science Research, Highly Sophisticated Research and, from 1995, Harmonic Science Research. The HSR-VI possessed 1997's daftest feature: if you chose 'driver-operated' mode rather than 'automatic pilot', the roof section rose when the car was in motion. It was explained in the accompanying Mitsubishi press material that this mechanical – ahem – erection was designed to 'express the pleasure of the driver when personally handling the car'.

24 Triumph TR7

Bad Sports

The TR7 hit the UK market in late 1974, hailed as the Leyland conglomerate's first genuinely new sports car in a decade and a half. Many other dramatic claims were made for the scallop-sided coupé, but the TR7's only substantial achievement was to make every back-yard kit-car maker feel like a fine craftsman.

The TR7 was built by a fast deconstructing British Leyland in the industrial nightmare that was 1970s Britain. Even the most sympathetic reviewers struggled to find positive words for the TR7's massive bumpers, the huge, heavy tail, and that gruesome crease along the side. And the styling, alas, was the high point.

Britain's *Motor* magazine performed a 12-month 19,312-km (12,000-mile) test on one example, and the car only just made it. By the end of the test, the car's drivetrain had been almost completely rebuilt under warranty, yet the car still had what the magazine described as 'disfiguring rust' and myriad other problems. 'A particularly nasty lemon' was the magazine's summation.

Triumph designers had aimed the car at the American market at a time when safety and emission regulations were changing drastically. In their attempt to solve a whole lot of new challenges from the bottom floor of the poisonous Leyland bunker, they ended up with a tintop when traditional TR buyers expected a convertible. And they ended up with a strict two-seater at a time when the four-seater ('two-plus-two') version of Datsun's Z-Car was outselling the standard version by four to one.

The TR7 was designed to look mid-engined, but its powerplant was in the nose. There were boasts of new aerodynamic benchmarks, but road testers complained of 'unbearable' noise at 126 km/h (78 mph). The TR7's barely adequate power was courtesy of a 2-litre 69-kW (92-bhp) four-cylinder engine borrowed from the Triumph Dolomite sedan. There was acceptable handling, to be just, and a five-speed manual transmission. But to the standard Triumph fare of

poor ventilation, dodgy controls, unreliable electrics, and dismal build quality, the TR7 added poor outward visibility in all directions, doors that simply didn't fit their openings, and – wait for it – tartan upholstery. Okay, that may not have been strictly speaking a fault. But it was certainly avoidable.

The TR7 went on sale in the United States in 1975, but eighteen months later almost a whole year's production was lost to strikes before production was moved from Liverpool to Coventry.

So desperate were the Australian marketers, they ran advertisements showing the TR7 as a double bed on wheels. The caption read: 'This is how your girlfriend's mother will view your new TR7.' Very daft indeed.

By the end of the 1970s, an open-top TR7 became available in the US and UK. Even a V8 version (TR8) saw slender light of day, but the game was up. Within a few years Triumph would go the way of Alvis, Austin, Morris, Riley, Wolseley, and all those other expired British Motor Corporation/Leyland brands.

25 Biscuter

A One-Pot Screamer

Despite its ultra-expensive misadventure with the exotic Pegaso, Spain's Empresa Nacional de Autocamiones SA (ENASA) soon returned to car-making. The second time around, the result was ultra-inexpensive and just a little less than exotic.

The major push (words not chosen by chance) was behind a thing known as the Biscuter, which means 'two-scooter'. This tiny four-wheeled chariot of ire might have looked as if it was styled by Noddy with a bit of help from Big Ears, but its origins actually rested with the French aeronautic pioneer Gabriel Voisin. He wanted to create a car even more basic than the Citroën 2CV, which itself came from a design brief famously stipulating 'four deckchairs under an umbrella'. Voisin could find no interest in France, so he sold Spain on the idea.

The Biscuter was powered (just) by a one-cylinder engine designed (badly) by Villiers and built (even badlier) by ENASA. The vehicle acquired the nickname Zapatilla, after the open slippers worn by peasants, and thanks to an almost complete lack of competition it became suspiciously close to popular. Production lasted from 1953 to 1960.

During a road test by the British magazine *The Motor*, a Biscuter broke down six times and recorded a fuel figure of 16 mpg (6.8 km/litre), against a claim of 'up to 63 mpg' (26.8 km/litre). The

journalist at the wheel, Richard Bensted-Smith, wrote: 'The greater part of the noise, smell and confusion live with the engine between the front wheels, which drive and, God willing, stop the machine at the behest of the driver sitting with as many friends (up to one and a half) as he can persuade to accompany him roughly amidships.' The magazine did not go on to recommend the Biscuter to readers.

26 Leyland P76

The End of an Error

Leyland P76. Anything but average.

In many ways the Leyland P76 was a good car. But, alas, in many more ways it was a bad one. The all-new big family car of 1973 was meant to save an already sick Leyland Australia, but it sold poorly, made an inglorious exit only fifteen months after launch, and took the rest of the company down the drain with it. Along the way it established a reputation as Australia's Edsel – and with good reason.

So what was good? The P76 was a big (well, huge) and comfortable family car with the option of an interesting alloy block 4.4-litre V8 engine, a donk developed from the Rover 3.5, in turn developed from a General Motors V8. The car boasted an aerodynamic wedge-shaped body, some advanced-for-the-day engineering features and – *drumroll, drumroll* – a boot large enough to accommodate a 44-gallon drum (this peculiar attribute was one of the most heavily publicised).

And what was bad? Where to start? The slogan was 'Anything but average', which proved to be sadly true. Every car seemed to have a unique combination of faults. The model number P76 came from the engineer's project number, itself arrived at when the Leyland supremo, Lord Stokes, read the code 'P76' from the back of his watch during a business meeting. It might have been more helpful, however, had Stokes taken note of some of the other terms on the back of his watch – such as 'dust-proof' and 'water-resistant'.

Even if people warmed to the P76 shape (and many didn't) and could live with its gargantuan size, they still had to put up with any combination of the following: rust, internal draughts blowing in from huge gaps in the panels and poor sealing, myriad squeaks and leaks, smouldering carpets (due to a poorly insulated exhaust system), interior fittings that shook loose, fast-deteriorating paint, and the choice between a six-cylinder engine that was an underperformer or the alloy V8 that went hard but was prone to overheat in traffic and in some cases to corrode internally. There were also windshields and side windows with an unnerving ability to come unstuck on rough roads, or even during heavy braking.

The joke was that when you delivered a P76 for warranty work, it was quicker to tell the mechanic the things that *didn't* need fixing. The car became popularly known as the P38 – only half the car it was supposed to be – but the problems were bigger than the P76 itself. Leyland was a hostage to bad management, hostile unions, national industrial policy that constantly changed without forewarning or apparent awareness of the consequences, severe budgetary problems, poor production design, and dud components from supplier companies experiencing the same sort of problems as Leyland itself. Worst of all, the company had launched the P76, a big car, during an energy crisis, and it was also a premium-priced model

in a time of severe inflation and deteriorating consumer confidence. And they had courageously done it all under a new badge, Leyland, rather than using Austin, Morris, or another handle familiar to Australians.

Despite all this, the V8 version won Australia's *Wheels* magazine Car of the Year award for 1973. The decision has embarrassed the magazine ever since but, to be completely fair, the call was made before all the quality glitches were apparent, and at a time when only locally built cars were eligible for the award. This made the field rather narrow. So narrow, in fact, that something built by Leyland during the 1970s could win.

Sales failed to pick up and a 'Force 7' coupé variant, complete with a novel hatchback rear door, was frantically readied for market in the desperate belief it could help save the farm. If Leyland Australia had survived, the Force 7 would have hit the market at the exact time the local divisions of GM, Ford and Chrysler were preparing to phase out their coupés because the daft fad for large cars with enormous doors and small interiors had passed.

Unlike the competing two-doors, which used existing front body panels to save production costs, the Force 7 uniquely had sheet-metal from nose to tail. The rush to get it to market had shown up severe – some say fatal – structural rigidity problems. Nonetheless, about sixty examples were sent down the line before Leyland hit the canvas. For reasons not entirely clear, all but ten were destroyed. The survivors – finished in such 1970s colours as Oh Fudge and Home on th'Orange – were auctioned off.

27 Cosmic Invader

Flat, Strapped

Yes, you guessed correctly: Carl Casper's battery-powered three-wheeled Cosmic Invader was built in the 1970s. Need we explain why it failed to outsell the Volkswagen Beetle?

28 Jensen-Healey

Not Even Nearly

For one brief shining moment it looked like salvation for the British
sports-car industry: a new two-seater roadster with a modern body, a
double-overhead-camshaft engine, and not one famous name on the
bodywork but two. It was the Jensen-Healey, and as an extra bonus in
the brand department, its alloy engine was made by Lotus. There was
only one small problem: the Jensen-Healey was one of the shoddiest
cars ever built.

Its gestation began in 1967, when the much-loved Healey 3000
ceased production because it was unable to comply with stricter US
safety and pollution laws. The British Motor Company declared that
the MGC (a horror of a six-cylinder MGB) would be the 3000's
successor, but Kjell Qvale, a millionaire Californian car dealer and
Anglo-sports-car fanatic, wanted a worthier replacement. He wanted it
so badly he bought out Jensen, the revered English sports-car builder
and coachmaker that had produced the Healey 3000 bodies.

In 1970 Qvale made Donald Healey (of Austin-Healey fame)
chairman of Jensen Motors Ltd and himself president. The Jensen-
Healey appeared two years later and the sheer joy of seeing an all-
new ragtop in depressed early 1970s Britain made the press rave. It
soon became obvious, however, that the car was underdeveloped
and the build quality obscene.

The Jensen-Healey was a bitza, which is to say it was made of bits of this and bits of that. Unfortunately, many of the borrowed components were not too flash to start with. The Vauxhall Viva steering assembly was prone to fail under the weight of its new obligations, and the Chrysler transmission, although modified, also struggled to cope. The engine was a 2-litre fed by big Dellorto carburettors, or Strombergs on some export versions. It put out a respectable 105 kW (140 bhp) and torque of 173 Nm (128 lbs/ft), though with levels of noise and unreliability that would become legendary.

How's this for stupid? Park an early J-H on a slope and the contents of the fuel tank would slip past the carbs and into the sump. Other vices, often less exotic but equally unforgivable, were found in every area of the engine, and most defied continuous updates and running changes. Many things that should have been kept inside the Jensen-Healey leaked out, while things that should have been kept outside leaked in. The fold-down roof was frustratingly complicated to operate and tended to lack that one feature we most expect in a roof: an ability to protect us from the elements.

The body was a monocoque (unitary construction type), which made Ye Olde Traditional English Rust even more of a problem. Water seemed to be able to find its way into the leg space and other parts via huge panel gaps, and many Jensen-Healeys were soon sagging in the middle. Reports also spread of camshafts seizing, water pumps failing, door locks falling into doors, and endless electrical peccadillos.

Of the 10,453 Jensen-Healeys built, 7,709 went to the United States. Also built were about 450 examples of a particularly ugly fixed-roof GT version. Production ceased in 1976, by which point Jensen was in receivership.

29 Arna

The Odd Coupling

Despite anything you may unkindly think, Arna was not the Roman god of poor panel fit or popped engine seals. It was an acronym of Alfa Romeo and Nissan Automotive and was the name given to a car that looked like a Nissan Pulsar with an Alfa grille. The year was 1983 and Alfa and Nissan each thought they had good reasons to jump in the sack and spawn this unique Japanese–Italian 'thorough-hybrid'.

The Arna gave Nissan access to Italy's car market (which was then mostly closed to imports), while the financially challenged Alfa gained financial assistance from the Far East plus metal you couldn't see through after six months. But the car itself, which promised to bring the best of both worlds, instead managed to combine Nissan's flair and road manners with Alfa's build quality and reliability.

The body panels – many of which were produced in Japan – were screwed together in Italy and the vehicle was fitted with an Alfa grille and a 1.2-litre version of the Alfa boxer engine. The Arna had an English sister, too, the daftly named Nissan Cherry Europe, which also 'benefited' from Alfa power.

So successful was the venture that Arna became a household name. The household in question was located next to the Arna plant in Pratola Serra near Avellino.

30 NSU Ro80

Floored Genius

Car of the decade. Machine of the future. The most significant automobile since the Second World War.

There seemed no praise too lavish for the stunning new NSU unveiled in Germany in late 1967. And some of the acclaim was justified. This front-drive, wedge-shaped exercise in advanced aerodynamics and improved packaging efficiency was truly revolutionary and set the tone for the so-called aero cars of the 1980s. Furthermore, the newcomer was fitted with a Wankel rotary engine, the smooth, compact, and powerful miracle motor that was poised to oust the standard reciprocating engine from its smug position of power.

Yes, the Ro80, built by the German company NSU-Automobil, was one of those cars that comes but once a generation and changes all that follows. The pity was that it also sent its manufacturer broke and left tens of thousands of owners enormously unhappy.

The Ro80 powerplant had a capacity of 995 cc (60.5 cubic inches), yet developed a comparatively huge 96 kW (128 bhp). That was the good news. The bad went beyond the unfortunate decision to name the engine after its designer, Felix Wankel. NSU was in financial trouble and the Ro80 had been rushed to market before the engineer's considerable concerns about mechanical durability had been fully addressed.

The Wankel proved thirsty, but the main problem was that the engine seals failed to properly seal the chambers created by the triangular rotor within the epitrochoidal housing in which it oscillated (you are following this, aren't you?). Engine failure at around 16,000 km (10,000 miles) and less was common. Around the world, NSU replaced thousands of engines free of charge. Unfortunately they replaced them with Ro80 engines. And the company wasn't completely 'mea culpa'; NSU apportioned much of the fault to poor maintenance and 'abuse of the free-revving nature of the Wankel engine'.

It was a particular shame because the Ro80 had so many virtues. Consider a few: a roomy cabin with a long flat floor, a clever clutchless semi-automatic transmission, a quietness and smoothness that was almost eerie, and a top speed of 175 km/h (over 108 mph). There was also excellent steering plus brilliant handling, powerful brakes, a standard of fit and finish that drew near universal praise, and styling that, love it or hate it, was as different and distinctive as that of any mainstream newcomer since the Citroën DS of the 1950s (it looks less radical now because, unlike the Citroën, it was widely imitated).

The Ro80 also had such unusual-for-the-1960s things as a heated rear window and a ski hatch in the rear seat. But the car's single most publicised feature – the revolutionary powerplant – was its failing. The Ro80 was a great meal brought to the table too quickly. If fitted with a conventional engine, or launched a couple of years later with a better version of the same engine, the NSU Ro80 very likely would have been an enduring success. After all, Mazda was soon to prove that the Wankel could at least be reliable, if never cheap to produce or fuel-efficient.

In late 1969, NSU was financially challenged (okay, bankrupt) and was taken over by VW-Audi. Ro80 production continued for another eight years, while many of the former NSU engineers helped refine and improve the concept for their new employer. Their efforts included the wind-cheating Audi 100CD of 1982. It was this conventionally powered Audi that finally realised the promise of the Ro80.

31 Ford Falcon 'Argentina'

Ropey Old Bird

Although Ford's publicity department didn't make a big deal of it, the first ever Falcon – sold in the US from 1959 – was alive and semi-well in the early 1990s and, in keeping with the cliché, living in Argentina.

The standard model gracing new car showrooms at the time had a 3-litre straight-six engine with an 'Argelite' down-draught carburettor and it boasted – a modest boast certainly – a 'three-speed fully synchronised gearbox'. There were saloon and station-wagon body styles, but it seems they no longer had a 'Squire' version with those wonderful fake wood strips attached to each flank.

As shown here, the Argentinians used brilliant tricks of the styling trade to almost totally disguise that their locally built Falcon wasn't a state-of-the-art design. By the time production was wound up in 1991 nearly half a million had been built – with little more than sheet-metal and cosmetic changes made to the original 1950s design.

32 Quasar

Boxing Stupid

When the science of aerodynamics swept the world, it somehow missed Middlesex, where the Quasar was built in 1968.

This cubular hell was the work of a British automotive parts supplier, Universal Power Drives Ltd, and was based on a design by Quasar Khanh, a North Vietnamese engineer living in Paris.

Six was the magic number, the Quasar being 6 feet wide, 6 feet long and 6 feet tall. It could also seat exactly that number of adults. One of the design briefs was 'complete transparency'. Bizarrely this ran to the seats which, perhaps uniquely in the history of the automobile, were made from inflatable see-through PVC plastic. And Khanh, it seems, thought other car-makers were paying not nearly enough attention to upward visibility, so he made the roof out of glass too. This enabled the driver to swerve if he or she noticed, for example, an intercontinental ballistic missile bearing down from the heavens.

The Quasar made use of sliding doors, so the occupants – if not already deep-fried by the sun or permanently stuck to the PVC seats – could park the vehicle in tight spaces and then exit easily. There was one sliding door on each side and one at the front, so the Quasar could also double as a patio/entertaining area. The 'body-work' was

manufactured from Triplex safety glass, and that single windscreen wiper looks capable of sweeping at least 3 per cent of it.

The press release noted that, 'Ideally the design would have incorporated electric motive power bringing about complete silence and eliminating smoke emission.' However, the design didn't. Power instead came from a British Motor Company 1.1-litre petrol engine, placed in the rear. Universal Power Drives described the top speed as 'restricted to 50 mph' [80 km/h]. In a car that isn't much, but in a glorified shower recess it sounds positively frightening.

The manufacturer boasted its 'exciting new creation' would become a popular city vehicle as it could turn in half the space of a family sedan. Looking at the shape, the high centre of gravity and the tiny 25.4 cm (10-inch) wheels, one suspects it could roll over much more quickly than the average family saloon too.

So how did it sell? In a word, badly. Despite claims that the Quasar was just what the world was waiting for, the world took a quick look at Universal Power Drive Ltd's peculiar display cabinet on wheels and signalled it was prepared to wait a little longer. A few Quasars went to the French textile group SNIP, for reasons not entirely obvious, and one was used in *She does not Drink, Smoke or Flirt, but . . . She Talks!*, a widely unapplauded French film from 1970.

33 Urbanina

Pisa's Lean Machine

A cross between a motor scooter and a car, with a cockpit that revolved for ease of parking, the Urbanina was conceived by a group of Italian designers from Pisa and unveiled at the 1965 Turin motor show. This so-called 'traffic beater' had a 175-cc (10.6-cubic-inch), 8.5-bhp (6.4-kW) engine, two seats, and excellent headroom. That said, the female in the motor show press photos – possibly the very person immortalised in the song 'The Girl from Urbanina' – seemed to be having trouble controlling the vehicle while stationary. Have pity on her and other road users if it really were to reach the claimed top speed of 60 mph (96.5 km/h).

Having identified an untapped market for a car with the weather protection of a scooter, the Urbanina successfully untapped it.

34 Rover SD1

Stay Rover, Leak Oil Rover, Play Dead Rover

In the late 1970s, there was no room for shoddy quality within the British Leyland organisation. This was because there was already so much shoddy quality within the British Leyland organisation they couldn't possibly fit any more in.

Against this rather depressing backdrop came the SD1 from British Leyland's Rover division. It was an innovative design that deserved a lot more. A lot more, for example, than being built by Rover during that era.

The SD1 (it stood for Specialist Division project 1) was first sold in 1976 and, like so many British cars of the era, had much to commend it. The big Rover introduced a totally new body concept to the luxury market (it was a hatchback) and had excellent handling. Its styling was bold and strikingly different; although not everyone liked it at the time, the lines have held up remarkably well.

Rover described the five-door as a 'midweek gentleman's express which transformed into a weekend family runabout'. So popular was the concept that the SD1 secured the European Car of the Year award for 1977, and initial sales on the home market exceeded expectations.

But that, ladies and gentlemen, was as good as it got. Reality was still to be faced and no sooner had Rover built up an order bank than the brand-new, purpose-made plant in Solihull went on strike, drastically cutting supply. Those people who received cars, however, were not necessarily the lucky ones.

In keeping with BL tradition, it wasn't too long before things started falling off. They were small things at first: switches, wipers, door handles. But then, increasingly, it was the big bits, the ones that made the car stop and go. There was the small matter of leaks, too, as the rear hatches of the early cars tended to let water in, and the engines and transmissions tended to let oil out. Electrically, it was a nightmare while the quality of the paintwork and fit-and-finish, marginal on day one, quickly nose-dived. Yes, alas, it was soon obvious that, despite the promising start, this was just another dog named Rover.

Soon after the Euro Car of the Year gong, one English car magazine awarded the SD1 its Worst Car of the Year appellation. A more forgiving journal, *Motor*, tested one and reported with apparent satisfaction, 'No major disasters, only a few minor trim and equipment failings.'

The engine was a 3.5-litre version of the alloy block V8, originally developed by Buick. This had powered such vehicles as the Leyland P76 and the original, grossly unreliable Range Rover (and, indeed, later grossly unreliable Range Rovers). The transmission choice was between a pig-heavy manual and a slushy three-speed auto.

A six-cylinder version followed, and this added camshaft failure to the long list of SD1 problems. Meanwhile, the Solihull plant continued to set ever higher benchmarks for days lost to strikes.

The SD1's reputation preceded it; when it was exported to Australia there was a rather mystifying paragraph in the press release about 'a detailed local development and modification programme' and a local 'quality upgrade'. There were very few cars in the world that could be improved by Leyland Australia.

The blackened name also ensured that the designation SD1 was not used. The model was referred to as the Rover 3500 V8 and received a whole lot of cheap plumbing to meet Aussie emission regulations. Not only did the early Australian-delivered Rover 3500 V8s have fearsome fuel consumption, they took a very leisurely 12 seconds to hit 60 mph from rest. The 'executive express' was more of an 'executive all stations'.

On the home front, the Rover went through several upgrades, and particularly with the Vanden Plas and Vitesse versions of the early 1980s, it came much closer to realising its original promise. But by then few people cared and an almost bankrupt Rover had been forced into a joint venture with Honda. When the SD1 was replaced in 1986, it was with a reskinned Honda Legend.

35 Datsun 280ZX

The Z-Z-Z Car

Once upon a time there was a svelte, low and exciting coupé badged as the Datsun 240Z. America's *Road & Track* magazine called it 'the most significant sports car of the '70s'. In just a few years, Datsun's best and brightest had turned this into the 280ZX. Hundreds of millions of yen and thousands of hours of intense development had turned a light, stylish, agile, quick and affordable coupé into one that was heavy, unattractive, lumbering, slow and expensive.

The 240Z was styled by ex-Studebaker designer Albrecht Graf Goertz and launched in 1970. It was half the price of the ageing E-Type Jaguar, but considerably more than half the car. The Zed's performance and handling left competitors such as the MGB in the shade. With the revamped 260Z, released in 1974, every major statistic had increased, including capacity, power and weight. An additional two-plus-two variant (which is to say a semi-four-seater) saw the overall length blow out even further. But it was the 280ZX of March 1979 that totally lost the plot. Not just bigger and heavier again, it was festooned with chrome galore, chintzy body decorations and seats covered in the sort of velour you'd find in a really bad 1970s nightclub.

The Zed was now two-plus-two only and Datsun was using the term 'personal coupé', as if no longer game to say 'sports car'. The bonnet seemed to go on for ever but it's hard to say why, since it hid an inline six-cylinder engine which produced just 98 kW (130 bhp) and was expected to propel nearly 1,300 kg (2,866 pounds), usually via a three-speed automatic. The slushbox option (the majority of Zed's were now auto), along with power windows, power mirrors and featherweight power-assisted steering showed that the Zed car was pitched at a very different buyer. The main reason for the switch from lean-and-mean to obese-and-serene was that, with 80 per cent of Zeds going to the USA, the car had been increasingly tailored to the, er, unique tastes of that market.

In 1980 a T-bar roof made the 280ZX a sort of semi-demi-convertible. And even heavier. By 1982 the 280ZX was officially a 'Nissan' and marketed as 'the only luxury hatchback coupé available with a targa roof'. Sports car – what's that?

36 Paykan

The Plight of the Hunter

The last Paykan sedan smoked, clunked and splattered off the end of the production line at the Iran Khodro plant, west of Tehran, in May 2005. The gala occasion, attended by Iran's industry minister Eshagh Jahangiri and involving ribbons, banners and excruciatingly long speeches, ended nearly forty years of production of a slow, boxy and badly built car that started life in Britain as a Hillman Hunter.

Paykan means arrow in the Farsi language. The first examples were produced in Iran under licence in 1967 and, rather like the East German Trabant, the car stayed well beyond its welcome and gave rise to a local culture of jokes (sample: Why don't Paykans sustain much damage in a front-end collision? The tow truck takes most of the impact.).

Due to low wages and prohibitive import duties, the Paykan was for many Iranians the only affordable set of wheels, and the final production tally was a staggering 2,295,095 units. When production ceased, the Paykan still accounted for one third of all cars on the country's roads and an equally large percentage of the nation's jokes. (One more: What do you call a Paykan with brakes? Customised.)

The combination of a dated design and worn-out tooling meant a 2005 Paykan used more fuel than most large luxury cars. One estimate put the average consumption at worse than 18 L/100 km, or 15.7 mpg. Such profligate drinking is less of a problem in oil-rich Iran than the large amounts of black smoke that pump out the other end. The Paykan has often been cited by Iranian officials as a reason Tehran is one of the most polluted cities in the world and residents are frequently hospitalised with respiratory complaints.

The loathsome build quality might have been due to more than clapped-out production machinery. It was widely believed in Iran, and possibly true, that the maker had a policy of collecting discarded Paykans and remachining the parts for use in new examples. (The last, I promise: What is found on the last two pages of the Paykan owner's manual? The bus schedule.)

Still, the simplicity of the old carburettored four-cylinder engine (originally a 1.7-litre, more recently a 1.6), and the basic nature of the other mechanical components have allowed owners to keep their Paykans going well beyond expectations and, in some cases, well beyond belief. Spare parts are abundant too, and body panels are cheap – a major advantage in Tehran traffic.

If not for an Islamic revolution then an eight-year war with neighbouring Iraq, the Paykan would likely have been phased out decades ago. By the time the last Paykan came off the line, Iran Khodro was already building versions of Peugeot's more modern 405 and even 206 models, though at a much higher price than the humble Paykan.

37 Packard Predictor

Harbinger of Doom

American nomenclatural know-how gave us such majestic handles as Eliminator, Mach 1, Turnpike Cruiser, Super Motion, and Packard's very own Predictor. This stunningly something machine was first displayed at the 1956 Chicago Motor Show and can possibly be linked to the demise of the Packard Motor Car Company soon after. It was a demise that the Predictor failed to predict.

Around 1954 the Packard company had made the decision to buy Studebaker, a daft idea that looked likely to guarantee that neither brand would last long. By 1956 Packard was already on the decline, having built only 10,000 cars for the year, compared with 116,000 in 1949. Being further weighed down by Studebaker's exceedingly inefficient manufacturing operations didn't help. The Packard–Studebaker concern was bought by Curtis-Wright Corporation just after the Predictor was shown, but the Packard brand dribbled to a stop circa 1958. The new owners managed to pick up and drag Studebaker into the 1960s, but the brand finally ran out of steam in 1966.

The Predictor featured hidden headlights and a grille that made the nose of the slightly later Edsel look almost understated. Added to this were dogleg A-pillars, a Ford Anglia-style reverse-rake roof, opera windows (each with a chrome flash through the centre), fins with high-

mounted aerials, and triangular tail-lights. The sliding roof panels were said to aid entry; with the benefit of hindsight they could possibly be considered a forerunner to the detachable-panel 'targa' roof. Then again, why give these people any credit?

38 FSM 650

Unpolished Pole

Known as the Nikko, Niki, Polski Fiat 126, and FSM 650 during its twenty-seven-year run, the automobile that Poles nicknamed Maluch ('the toddler') was the result of a deal between the Polish state and Fiat in the very early 1970s.

The first models – made in Bielsko-Biala, south of Warsaw – came off the line in 1973, and during the 1980s examples increasingly turned up in Western countries. This was mainly because Fiat had stopped producing the original 126 in Italy, believing there was no longer a market for such a crude and basic car.

That belief was quickly proved wrong and Fiat soon started buying back up to 45,000 Polish-built 126s each year to sell on its home market alongside its supposed replacement, the Panda hatchback.

The Polish 126 was built by FSM. This stood for Fabryka Samochodow Malolitrazowych, which rolled off the tongue as gracefully as this pensioned-off design took to the road.

How the FSM 650 passed Western safety and emission laws into the 1990s was never fully explained. The engine, which hung over the back axle, was a 652-cc (40-cubic-inch), air-cooled, two-cylinder, carburettor-fed screamer with a manual choke that, if not used judicially, would flood the engine. Flood the engine? What was this . . . an automobile or a lawn mower?

In the early days you could have any colour you liked, as long as it was bleak. It was a peculiarity of the Eastern Bloc that cars were painted in the most drab hues ever devised to guard against inspiring consumerist passion in citizens. However, as exports grew the colour choice improved and, supposedly, so did the quality. Which leads to the frightening thought of what it was like before they raised it to 'still nowhere near acceptable'.

The measuring tape showed the 650's overall length was 3.1 metres (10.5 feet). That made it about half a metre shorter than any other four-wheeler on most markets during the 1980s, while its weight of 600 kg (1,320 pounds) was similarly other-worldly. Third-worldly, in fact. The engine put out just 18 kW (24 bhp), so to keep up with city traffic you had to bury the right foot and adjust your speed with the gearbox. Gaps in traffic had to be second-guessed in advance, otherwise you weren't going through. Momentum was everything. The noise was indescribable. And, thanks partly to Polish-made Stomil tyres, the 650 changed direction like a shopping trolley. Only less precisely.

'The fully imported 650 has a rear-mounted engine which gives you Porsche-like roadholding ability,' said one English-language brochure, written by someone who clearly had never driven it. In reality, Poland's Fiat demonstrated every handling vice known to suspension engineers, plus some invented especially for this car.

The options list had 'not available' next to air-conditioning, automatic transmission, and power steering. What you saw was what you got: flipper-style front windows, a single-speed interior fan, drum brakes all round, a non-synchromesh manual transmission. There was

not even a glove compartment or radio. The four seats had scarcely enough padding for one. The offset driving position was somewhere between Alfaesque and Kafkaesque.

On the plus side, it was very cheap. In Australia, for example, the Aus $7,990 price tag made it exactly $10 cheaper than the leather seat trim option on a Porsche 928. In the UK even the later, water-cooled 700-cc version with a lift-up rear hatch (known as the 126 BIS) was priced at just £2,688 in 1988. That made it half the price of some other small cars and only 2.4 per cent of the cost of a new Rolls-Royce Corniche.

The 650's speedometer was usually calibrated to 140 km/h or 85 mph, but attempts by Western car magazines to record a 0-to-100 km/h (61 mph) acceleration time faltered because the car wouldn't reach the desired speed in the available space. By the time 80 km/h (50 mph) came up, over 30 seconds had elapsed. But don't think the lack of power added up to particularly special economy. Indeed, if there was anything to recommend this pocket-size horror, no serious road tester found it.

In Poland, the production of the 126 BIS stopped in 1992. However, the air-cooled 650 continued to stumble off the production line until the year 2000. By then over 3 million had been made, none of them well.

39 Pininfarina Diamond Car

Hardly a Jewel

Complete with Cadillac-height fins, what looks like a rear roofline from a Citroën Goddess, and a wheel at each of its oddly placed extremes, Pininfarina's Diamond Car was one of the celebrated Italian design house's least celebrated creations. 'Diamond' referred in this case to the wheel layout: one each at the front and back, one on the left, one on the right.

Built in 1960, it was powered by a rear-mounted 1.1-litre engine, although information was scant on whether this was supplying power to one, two, three, or four wheels. Advantages of putting the road wheels in places where at least half would miss the tracks on the average garage hoist were claimed to include low torsional stresses, light weight, and reduced production costs.

The idea of a diamond wheel layout excited almost no serious interest in its day, and has continued to do so ever since.

40 Stutz Blackhawk

A Touch of Crass

The name Stutz seems to spring straight out of the pages of an F. Scott Fitzgerald novel. The revered brand, founded by Harry K. Stutz, had a lineage going right back to the earliest Indianapolis 500 races, and Stutz produced elegant speedsters and sumptuous luxury cars through the 1920s and into the 1930s.

It has even been claimed that the Stutz automobile was such an integral part of the American success story during the 1920s that if anyone committed suicide in one, or otherwise managed to kill themselves behind the wheel, they would automatically rate an obituary in the *New York Times*.

None of this illustrious history, however, has anything to do with an ostentatiously ugly vehicle produced three and a bit decades after the original Stutz company filed for bankruptcy. The story goes that in 1968 James O'Donnell, an investment banker, discovered that Stutz was listed as an 'unclaimed corporate name'. He wasted no time in making it a claimed corporate name.

Investment banking was obviously treating Mr O'Donnell well because the offices of the new Stutz Motor Car Company Inc. were in New York's Rockefeller Center, and the famed (rather than, say, tasteful) stylist Virgil Exner was soon engaged to design a new car wearing the famous nameplate. Exner had some experience with

exhumations. He had styled a new Duesenberg for a failed 1966 revival of that brand (Duesenberg, like Stutz, never really recovered from the Great Depression).

The new Stutz firm displayed its Blackhawk in 1969, and no one lacked an opinion on the styling. Fake side pipes, boot lid-mounted spare, faux running boards, two-tone paint, an ostentatious grille and outrageous expanses of chrome were all crammed on to a car that was, deep below, a plain old Pontiac Grand Prix. The interior was filled with exotic materials, including fur carpet and outlandishly costly woods and leathers. Buyers received custom-tailored luggage that matched both the interior upholstery and fur-lined boot.

The standard General Motors V8 engine was modified to produce a claimed, though hard to believe, 400 bhp (approximately 300 kW). The body was hand assembled in Italy by Carrozzeria Padana of Modena, where twenty-two coats of hand-rubbed '$100-a-gallon' lacquer were applied. Coupé, convertible, and limousine versions were built, bearing such monikers as Bearcat, Diplomatic Sedan, and Royale Limousine. All were variations of the one design. To gain an idea of the scale, consider that those monstrous front and rear overhangs ensured that even the shortest Stutz was around 5.9 metres (19.5 feet) from nose to tail.

In the States the Stutz price list started at $22,500 and proceeded up the scale to 'as much as you'd like to pay'. Mink carpet was listed among the accessories. The starting price meant that even the 'cheap' versions were among the most expensive cars of the day. To maintain exclusivity even further (as if the styling wasn't enough), the new company charged US$8 for its brochures. That was no small amount in 1970.

Elvis Presley, Muhammad Ali, and Sammy Davis Jr. – none of whom were associated with understated tastes – were said to be in the early rush of high-profile purchasers, though one suspects there wasn't exactly an onslaught of others. Nonetheless, a small number of modern Stutz cars made it abroad, including one or two to the UK.

By 1971, the reborn Stutz company had changed hands, and neither the new owner nor those who followed seemed to be meticulous record keepers. The most reliable production numbers suggest that about fifty cars were made in the first four years – though, amazingly, the company struggled on through the 1970s and even into the 1980s. A 1976 convertible called the Stutz d'Italia was listed as the most expensive car in the world at US$129,000, although Associated Press noted at the time that 'business isn't exactly booming'.

By one report the final Stutz was built as late as 1995. For whom, or why, is not clear.

41 AMC Pacer

Wide off the Mark

Marketing textbooks define durable goods as consumer products that are typically used over an extended period and can survive repeated uses. The AMC Pacer was neither durable nor good.

What American Motors called 'the first wide small car' appeared in mid-1975 and was grossly overweight, surprisingly tight on elbow room (despite possessing considerable girth), prone to cooking its

occupants under that huge greenhouse, and diabolical in the handling stakes. Other than that, there weren't too many problems, except, of course, that it was shoddily screwed together and ugly. Really, really ugly. And if googly eyes and a ridiculously bulbous tail with a huge overhang over the side of each rear wheel weren't enough, the Pacer was expensive to build and buy, and despite its so-called subcompact dimensions, it guzzled fuel.

The short bonnet was originally shaped for a GM-built Wankel engine. When this plan was stillborn, AMC engineers instead jammed in their hefty and well-aged six, making the Pacer as agile as an ocean liner and as desirable as gout.

42 Pegaso

Fascist Ferrari

Spain has never been a high-profile car maker. For a brief patch in the early 1950s, however, the country threw off its automotive anonymity and produced the Pegaso, one of the world's most expensive sports cars. The publicity was enormous, the reviews enthusiastic. If there had been buyers as well, it might have changed everything for the Spanish industry.

The background to Spain's brief bathing in the supercar limelight rests with the fascist government of General Francisco Franco and its sudden and mysterious delusions of automotive grandeur. In the wake of the Second World War (which Spain, battered by its civil conflict of the 1930s, opted out of), most Spanish car makers produced micros and trikes. These were the only powered vehicles the greater part of the impoverished population could afford. So it was a particular surprise when Empresa Nacional de Autocamiones SA (ENASA) unveiled the Pegaso coupé at the 1951 Paris Motor Show.

State-owned and known foremost as a builder of buses and trucks, ENASA had centred the unlikely new project around a complex V8 engine developed by Dr Wilfredo Ricart, a Spaniard who had previously worked for Alfa Romeo. The first Pegaso, the Z102, was an exquisitely crafted coupé with a 2.5-litre all-alloy quad-cam V8, Grand Prix-style suspension, and a top speed of 242 km/h (145 mph). That

PEGASO

El coche para el automovilista apasionado

was its standard specification; for those who thought it too slow, a supercharger was available.

The Z102 was built with little regard for cost, the government treating the process as 'training in excellence' for the ENASA engineers who would soon take on the world. Prices reflected the lavish approach. The most expensive Pegaso was four times the cost of a Mercedes 300SL, itself well beyond the reach of almost any Spaniard at that time.

Within a few years there were 3.2- and 4.7-litre versions of the same 90-degree V8 engine and no less than six completely different body styles. These bodies were drawn by leading French and Italian design houses but built in Spain. Coupés and convertibles were

produced, some boasting understated elegance, others showing ludicrously finned 1950s excess. The premium Pegaso, with supercharged 4.7-litre engine, had a claimed top speed of 266 km/h (160 mph) and was heralded as 'Europe's most powerful car'. By the mid-1950s work began on a Pegaso family saloon, but it never made it to the showrooms.

In 1957 the whole thing ground to a halt for reasons as mysterious as those that had caused production to start in the first place. ENASA went back to commercial vehicle production, having built just 130 Pegasos in six years, and having lost millions of dollars on a Franco folly.

43 Moskvich

The Little Wagon That Couldn't

This is an estate version of the Moskvich, a Russian saloon that owed its popularity to there being almost no competition.

The Soviet government's Tass news agency – which also got by without a lot of competition – described the five-door variant as an exciting highlight of the Technica-Aesthetics-Progress Exhibition held in the Standards Pavilion at the USSR Economic Achievements

Exhibition of 1970. Certainly the observers captured here are nearly beside themselves with excitement.

At around the same time, there was an attempt made to sell the Moskvich saloon in Australia. It lost just a little of its momentum when the evaluation model was loaned to Sydney-based British journalist Pedr Davis for a second opinion. On the first morning it refused to start. The following night it spontaneously combusted in his suburban driveway. Davis gave the potential importer a second opinion, and found time to offer a third and fourth as well.

Meanwhile, Tass said the estate's clever design allowed the rear seat to be folded 'within five minutes'. It also stressed the newcomer was attractive and safe, *attractive* and *safe* presumably being the Russian words for unsightly and exceedingly dangerous.

44 Cony Guppy

Small Fry

Generally, the Japanese car industry has managed to keep the emphasis on its successes, which have been many. But there were many early shockers, from the rebuilt English and French cars of the 1950s (from Nissan, Hino, and others) to entirely home-grown atrocities such as the three-wheeled Daihatsu Bee.

One of this writer's favourites – perhaps, I'll confess, because of the altogether ridiculous name – is the Cony Guppy from the early 1960s. The Cony Guppy was the work of the Nagoya-based Aichi Machine Industry Co. Ltd., which had developed from the Aichi Aircraft Co., which, according to a corporate profile from 1961, had been engaged in the manufacture of aircraft for the Japanese Navy 'before the war'.

As with so many Japanese company chronologies, Aichi's successes 'before the war' were followed by more successes 'after the war'. Strangely though, Aichi seemed to have done nothing in between these two periods. By the 1950s it made the decision to try its corporate hand at making automobile components, and then at manufacturing complete vehicles. In 1962 it delivered to an expectant world the Cony range of cars, which included this microscopic trucklet known as the Guppy.

The Guppy brochure came complete with an overlay sheet covered in brightly coloured fish. (Both cony and guppy are types of fish, though they are not found together, since one is saltwater, the other, fresh. Cony is also an Old English word for simpleton – but I digress.) Unusual for early 1960s Japan, the Guppy brochure showed women behind the wheel.

The initial powerplant had one cylinder and a thimble-size capacity of 199 cc. It developed a claimed 7 kW (9.3 bhp). It was described as four-stroke in some literature, and two-stroke elsewhere. This micromotor was mid-mounted, leaving the feet of the driver and passenger to hang over the front axle and double as some sort of early warning system for an impending crash. The road wheels looked as though they had been borrowed from a lawn mower, while the front-opening 'suicide' doors looked impossibly thin, flimsy, and, well, suicidal.

A delivery van variant with a 360-cc engine was sold as the Cony Giant, a '360' minitruck version followed (the Cony Wide, of course). There was also a variety of particularly unstable-looking Cony three-wheelers. The three-wheeler didn't seem to have a snappy name, but if the Giant and Wide protocol was followed, it clearly should have been known as the Cony Untippable.

Production of four-wheeled Cony vehicles peaked at about 1000 a month. In 1965 the Aichi company was absorbed by Nissan, and Cony brand cars went the way of so many other Japanese lost causes. The Aichi Machine Industry Co. name resurfaced again in 1997 when it was announced that the 'Nissan affiliate which assembles vehicles, and makes parts at its Nagoya plant' was to spin off its Aichi 'electric vehicle department'. Unfortunately, little more on the matter was heard and we were never given a name for the supposed Aichi-built electric car. Anyway, Cony Guppy was always going to be a hard act to follow.

45 Nissan Cedric

Lost in Translation

Who was responsible for calling a car Cedric, and what the hell was he thinking?

The answer to the first question is Katsuji Kawamata, the Nissan/Datsun supremo from 1957. He was thinking, apparently, that in Western markets 'Cedric' would bring to mind the image of a worldly, well-educated, upper-class English gentleman. Rather than, say, a lisping fop in a cravat with a slightly disturbing fondness for his mother.

Kawamata and his strange streak of Anglophilia also combined to give us Datsun's Bluebird badge, perhaps inspired by the record-breaking antics of Sir Malcolm Campbell. And when he saw the Lerner-Loewe musical *My Fair Lady*, Kawamata-san decided the Pygmalion transformation of a dirty flower girl into a beautiful princess was exactly what his engineers had achieved when they put a roadster body on the chassis of a frumpy little Datsun truck. The Fairlady badge was born.

The Cedric, styled like a small-scale 1950s Chevrolet with dogleg windscreen pillars and fins, went on sale in Japan in 1960, and a few were sold overseas over the next half a dozen years (as many as nineteen went to the US, for example). Despite failing to set the West alight, the Cedric badge survived on in the Japanese market into the

21st century. In the meantime, many compatriot brands joined in the stupid name game. Examples included Mazda's Bongo Brawny and Proceed Marvie, Honda's Today Humming and Mitsubishi's Debonair Exceed Contega. But perhaps the masterstroke of silly Japanese nomenclature was the Subaru Touring Bruce.

A slightly tarted-up version of the 1993 Legacy/Liberty wagon, it was named after actor Bruce Willis, presumably on the agreement it was never sold, or even mentioned, outside Japan. The promotional material, included billboards that quoted Bruce Willis as saying, 'I tried the Legacy.' Nice work if you can get it: he didn't even have to finish the sentence with something like '. . . and it was adequate.'

46 HDT Director

Alternative Energy Vehicle

The Director was the last, ugliest and altogether silliest car produced by HDT Special Vehicles, the partnership between GM's division in Australia, Holden, and that country's best-known domestic racing driver Peter Brock. Up until 1986 the union had turned out highly desirable performance versions of the local Opel-derived Holden Commodore under the slogan 'We Build Excitement'. And Brock had used Holden products to win the country's most celebrated motor race, the annual touring car enduro at Bathurst, no less than eight times.

But in 1986 strange stories started spreading. It was whispered that Brock had experienced a dramatic change of personality and that this widely idolised, no-nonsense driver was suddenly talking of gurus and crystals and magical energy sources. 'Brockie' had indeed invented what he was calling the 'Energy Polarizer', in league with his wife Beverley and a chiropractor named Eric Dowker. The troika was demanding that one be fitted to every HDT model.

The Polarizer was a sealed box that was small enough to fit in your hand. A Brock company brochure claimed it 'causes all molecules in its sphere of influence to be aligned or polarized . . . the overall effect is to reduce overall vehicle noises . . . achieve greater efficiency of the power train and steering systems, improving the engine and suspension performance'.

So confident was Brock that in early 1987 he announced a new model supposedly designed to take advantage of the Polarizer. It was the HDT Director, at an exalted Aus$60,000. Holden executives claimed they were not allowed to see, let alone test, this new model and couldn't support the extravagant claims made for it. They were concerned, no doubt, that if an owner felt his or her car's molecules were not being properly aligned by the new technology, it could make for some difficult arguments at the Holden dealer warranty counter.

Furthermore, the Director's body, a DIY effort clad with brutally clumsy fibreglass panels, made sin look quite attractive. Fans and even some motoring journalists wanted to be true believers, if only to

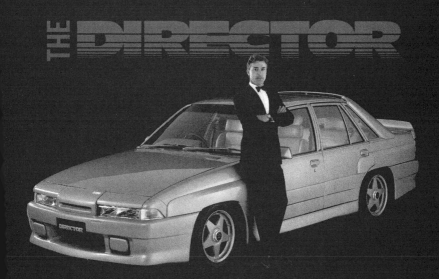

spare their hero the embarrassment. Alas, it soon transpired that the Polarizer worked rather like any other box of crystals and magnets held on by a single screw and expected to gather external energy via a metallic window sticker.

GM severed the business relationship and told Brock if he wanted to sell Commodores he could buy them at full price and supply his own warranty. The Director price immediately escalated and, considering everything, it's a miracle that Brock sold any, let alone 'not many'.

Unable to make a go of the Commodore business on his own, Peter Brock decided that the solution was modifying Russian-built Ladas for the Australian market. This time around Brock wasn't rebuilding the cars to improve performance but to prevent them falling apart. It was reputedly costing about $2,000 per car (then about £800) for the renamed Brock Organisation to bring brand-new off-the-boat Lada Samaras to a state that was acceptable to Australian car buyers. Very, very undiscerning buyers, that is.

The 'Brock' Samara was launched at a shade under $11,000 (sans Polarizer), but its price went into freefall as word-of-mouth caught up with it. The official slogan was 'Value is Everything', but a more honest approach would have been to adapt the HDT motto and announce, 'We Build Excrement'.

'From this springboard we will be taking some exciting steps forward,' Brock had said at the mid-1988 launch. A few months later he sold out his interest and bid the Lada people goodbye. The initial talk had been of 500 units per month. The reality was a trickle and Brock soon turned to modifying Ford Falcons instead.

47 Lightburn Zeta Sports

Extra Light

The Zeta Sports came one year after the lamentable Zeta Saloon and, perhaps more importantly, five years after the Australian-designed Goggomobil Dart.

Dart similarities included the tiny exterior dimensions, door-less fibreglass body and rear-mounted two-stroke engine. That the moment for such a vehicle had passed might have been hinted at by the disappearance of the Dart from radar screens. But South Australian cement-mixer-manufacturer/would-be car-magnate Harold Lightburn would not be deterred.

The body styling of the Zeta Sports came from Michelotti of Italy via an English company that had built a similar vehicle (called the Frisky Sprint) in the late 1950s, and had deservedly gone belly-up.

Power – a modest 15.5-kW (20.5-bhp) – was delivered by a '500-cc Continental two-stroke engine'. The term Continental was not a brand-name but a generic term for something European that couldn't be described by the then favourable term 'British'. The donk was a two-cylinder Sachs FMR powerplant from Germany, equipped with an integral four-speed gearbox. Because the Sports weighed just 400 kg (882 pounds), top speed was claimed as 75 mph (around 120 km/h), which sounds terrifying.

In the brochure for 'The exhilarating Zeta Sports', terms such as 'train-like cornering' and 'back-thumping acceleration' were liberally and ludicrously used. Yet – surprise, surprise – the new Zeta was

no supercar. The only thing it could leap in a single bound was out of gear.

The Sports sat on Mini-Minor-sized 25.4-cm (10-inch) wheels and had drum brakes and a single windscreen wiper. The body was bumper-less, with protruding headlights ready to take the brunt of any impact. Alas, these headlights proved to be too low to comply with some Australian state legislation. The first solution attempted was to raise the suspension, but the ground-hugging Zeta couldn't be raised far enough, and so cars were delivered with an extra set of 'sports lights' bolted on to the guards above the normal ones. Ugly and silly suddenly became uglier and sillier.

That as many as fifty Zeta Sports models were produced is surprising. That Lightburn Automotive Division built its last Zeta of any description in 1965 is not.

48 Rolls-Royce Camargue

Rolls of Fat

The arrival of a new Rolls-Royce is hardly a common occurrence, yet when 1975 brought that very thing there were more groans than (restrained and dignified) leaps of joy.

Although described as the last word in high tech (which, incidentally, is 'tech'), the new Camargue was merely a rebodied R-R Silver Shadow with a bit of extra equipment, including the forerunner to climate-control air-conditioning and that audio inanity of the 1970s, the eight-track cartridge player.

The Camargue – named after an area in southern France with which the car had no connection whatsoever – was billed as a 'two-door fixed-head coupé'. This was a subtle way of indicating it had many of the disadvantages of a convertible without any of the pleasures of a roof that could be taken down. Worse still, the Camargue was packaged in an awkward, angular body (styled by Italian design house Pininfarina) that looked more like an obese kit-car conversion than a coach-built masterwork.

Pointedly, the Camargue reinforced that its builder had reached the end of the familiar road. With the low volumes being achieved by Rolls-Royce in the 1970s and the crimping of the research and development budget that came as a result, the crew from Crewe no longer had any chance of building a better car than Mercedes-Benz

and others. This was particularly true when so much of Rolls-Royce's comparatively meagre R&D budget now had to be directed towards meeting ever more rigorous government legislation.

Rolls-Royce clearly had to trade on elegance and exclusivity, yet the Camargue brought only the second of these – and it was an exclusivity a lot more extreme than planned. Just 534 Carmargues (including 8 prototypes and test vehicles) were built over an eleven-year period.

The boxy outer skin, hand-crafted by Rolls-Royce's long-time coach-builder Mulliner Park Ward, was a good pointer to that of the forthcoming Silver Spirit saloon, another fatty that once again would repackage the familiar mechanical configuration of a 90-degree pushrod V8 powering the rear wheels via a three-speed automatic transmission. Maximum speed for the Camargue was listed as 122 mph, or just under 200 km/h. It was reputed to be the first Rolls-Royce designed to metric dimensions and the first in which the grille was angled for a more sporty look (a very slight angle, it must be said).

When launched in 1975 at just under £30,000, the Camargue was said to be the most expensive production car in the world. By 1986 the Camargue was still available on special order at something over £80,000. Takers were few.

At least the American magazine *Motor Trend* was positive, saying: 'There are cars which will accelerate faster, there are some which will handle better; there are even one or two which, in specific circumstances, are even quieter. But in this writer's opinion, there are none which can rival the Carmargue's ability to transport its occupants in such splendid isolation.' Most other journals were content to marvel at the 'automatic air-conditioning system' that allowed the driver to select a chosen temperature. A complex network of sensors did their best to maintain the set choice; the unit would even give different temperatures for the upper and lower parts of the interior.

Within that modest total of 534 Camargues was one Bentley-badged version, built for a customer who wanted to be doubly exclusive – and clearly wasn't too concerned about resale.

49 Triumph Mayflower

Reduction to the Absurd

More an Adversity than a Triumph, the Mayflower was a ludicrous attempt to graft the bodywork and associated grandeur of a large and powerful British limousine on to a small and powerless Triumph chassis.

Introduced in 1949, the Triumph Mayflower acquired nicknames such as 'the watch-charm Rolls-Royce', plus many things much less kind. The vehicle was apparently created to appeal to Americans, as was the opportunistic name. It was assumed they held English limousines in high regard and therefore would go for the same thing in a concentrate.

Unfortunately, nobody asked the Americans what they thought before production commenced, and Triumph ended up shipping only a few more Mayflowers to the New World than the original Pilgrims had in 1620. The company came to its senses in 1953 and abolished the model, then wrote it out of most official corporate histories.

50 Fascination

With radical wheel layout, miracle engine, and styling so far ahead of its time that we're still not ready for it, the Fascination lived up to its name. Mind you, it could have equally lived up to several other names, including Hopeful, Ludicrous and Daft.

It was in early 1973 that the Fascination was announced, with its American maker, the Highway Aircraft Corporation (HAC, a syndicate of American investors), calling it 'Tomorrow's Car Today'. It turned out to be more a case of tomorrow's car tomorrow, or perhaps the day after. Or never.

Amazing claims were made in lavish brochures and full-page newspaper advertisements. Readers were told that the Fascination was 'low cost, economical, safe, smog-free, modernistic, quiet, easy-to-handle and easy-to-park'.

It was the brainchild of one Paul Lewis of Sidney, Nebraska. The 'smog-free' claim was based on HAC having an option on a 'new, revolutionary, smog-free, boilerless steam engine' being developed by – stop me if you've heard this before – the Boilerless Steam Engine Corporation. While this powerplant was being readied, the Fascination would be available with a 52-kW (70-bhp) Renault 'four'. Thanks to the 'patented aerodynamic shape' this four-cylinder powerplant would somehow enable the Fascination to achieve '100 mph and 40 mpg' (160 km/h and 16.5 km/litre).

Showing a stronger grasp of hyperbole than of practical car design, HAC claimed the Fascination was 'the type of car millions of buyers want'. Acceptance by the public would be 'instantaneous because of the new and improved features and its perfectly streamlined beauty'. The vehicle's unique front-wheel design (the technical spec sheets described the Fascination as using 'single or dual guide wheels'), would triple tyre life. The vehicle would be so stable that overturning would be almost impossible.

Highway Aircraft Corporation announced that production would start in the United States, then expand to other countries. By March 1973 HAC claimed to have signed up thirty-six American dealers, but, strangely, no production cars were delivered in that year, nor in any of the years that immediately followed.

Nevertheless, various people were still labouring to put the car on the road. One was a Los Angeles-based inventor, Edwin V. Gray, a man who claimed to have been working for over twenty years on what

he called the Electro-Magnetic Association engine. Gray announced his powerplant to the world in 1973, at the time of the first energy shock, the very moment when the Fascination people were finding that the world wasn't exactly beating a path to their door. Gray claimed his engine harnessed static electricity and thereby could answer all the world's power needs, with no fuel use and, thanks largely to its cool running, virtually no wear.

The Fascination people announced Gray's engine would replace their boilerless steam engine. Not that they'd produced a boilerless steam engine or sold an actual car. Fascination press releases now headlined '$6 Million Fund Raised to Perfect the World's First No-Fuel Engine'.

From there it descends into a standard conspiracy-theory story. Neither the Los Angeles County district attorney's office nor the Securities and Exchange Commission believed statements made in the prospectus. Raids were conducted and Gray claimed that during these raids all his drawings and prototypes were confiscated. 'There has been a lot more to the suppression of my ideas than meets the eye,' said Gray, not at all paranoid.

Hereafter, it gets a little harder to follow. A 1977 press release announced that EBCO Inc. had entered into a contract with HAC to manufacture the 'Fascination Space Age Transportation Innovation'. By 1981, the same car was being referred to as the 'Fascination by Spencer Industries'. The only thing that remained constant was that you couldn't buy one. That said, at least one (presumably a Renault-powered prototype completed around 1974) actually did make it on to the road and is reportedly now in the hands of an American collector.

51 Ford Gyron

Putting on the Spin

In 1961 Ford engineers announced they had cleverly used a gyroscope to stabilise a two-wheeled car. But they forgot to tell us why. The advantages of compactness that might – just might – be realised with such an unusual arrangement were completely lost in the ridiculous bodywork. The 'delta-shaped' Gyron was a limousine-like 5.3 metres (17 feet 4 inches) in length, and more than 2 metres (6 feet 6 inches) wide. Yet it transported just two people.

Ford's head stylist called the Gyron 'an outstanding example of the visioneering that is the heart of progressive automotive styling'. All these years later, it still isn't known what the hell he was talking about.

The overall design concept, according to more gobbledygook from the styling team, was to break the link between the car and the carriage that preceded it; to use a starting point other than a square

machine with a wheel at each corner. Features included a steering dial with separate inner rings to control the speed and direction of travel. This apparently allowed the vehicle to be driven from either seat.

And did the Ford move in mysterious ways? Er, no. It didn't really move at all, as the small print in the press release revealed. 'Although the car is not operable in its present form, Ford stylists have been assured that a gyroscope no larger than two feet in diameter would be sufficient to stabilize the vehicle on its two wheels set in tandem.'

Even then, the Gyron required two small outrigger wheels at the rear to stabilise it while the gyroscope built up sufficient revs. Daft? You bet.

52 Honda S600

Cheap Shrill

First seen in Japan in 1964, the S600 sportster provided a superb example of how a large number of good ideas can be brought together and fused to create one very bad one.

It was the first Honda car to be exported in reasonable numbers and to some foreigners it seemed to be entirely in keeping with Japan's long tradition of miniaturisation. Others, however, argued that rather than being a shrunken car the micro two-seater was actually an enlarged motorcycle. It had chain-drive, for goodness sake, and pistons the size of pinheads, which broke the sound barrier inside a matchbox-sized engine that idled at 40,000 rpm.

Okay, there was an exaggeration or two in that past sentence. But the S600 did have chain drive. The tachometer was red-lined at a stunningly high 12,500 rpm. Because there was no form of rev limiter, many owners saw the engine hit 14,000 rpm and more – a sight often followed by a loud noise, then silence.

Two versions were sold: a convertible and, later, a coupé. Problem one was that the Honda was fiendishly expensive to produce and bore a retail price dangerously close to that of 'proper' English roadsters such as the Austin-Healey Sprite, which had full-size engines. A handful of S600s made it to the UK (including a couple of racing versions), but the lack of a left-hand-drive version meant it never officially made it to the States. The main export market was Australia, where one Honda executive claimed that the company would one day be 'as big a name in cars as it is in motorbikes'. Even the man who said it probably didn't really believe it. Dealers who had enjoyed success with Honda bikes turned up their noses. Many sports-car aficionados laughed.

Highly strung is the phrase that comes to mind. The S600 had a four-cylinder, water-cooled, twin-overhead-camshaft engine with four carburettors. Screaming its 600-cc (36.5-cubic-inch) head off, this madly complex motor pushed out a feisty 43 kW (57 bhp), giving the S600 a claimed top speed of 140 km/h (87 mph). But, as one mechanic put it, 'You could hear it wearing out.' What Honda considered a mini-masterpiece was unable to hang on to its roller bearings, was prone to rid itself of its oil, and, thanks to its motorcycle-style drive arrangements, became a champion at tearing up differentials. The S600 also regularly burned out its distributor points

and suffered a myriad other mechanical ailments. And, not surprisingly, the average owner didn't follow the handbook's rather inconvenient suggestion that the engine be warmed up for five minutes at 3,000 rpm before the car was driven.

The S600's rear-wheel-drive layout and four-wheel independent suspension helped ensure good handling. Though the brakes were drums all round, they worked extremely well with such a light package, and the fuel economy was excellent. Furthermore, the convertible version had a novel solution to wind noise: the shriek of the engine and chatter of the chains completely drowned it out.

A spate of early engine seizures in Australia prompted the local importers to do their own testing. They realised that they were very lucky it was only a spate rather than, say, an entirety. Honda in Japan responded by sending out a team of eight technicians. Working in white gloves, to the amusement of locals, they replaced the engine in every single S600 in the country. Such an extreme reaction and fanatical attention to detail was part of the reason Honda did indeed become as big a name in cars as it was in motorcycles. But there was still a long way to go and many more horrible automotive misjudgements in store.

At the 1966 Earls Court Motor Show a Honda convertible with an 800-cc engine and most of the other features of the S600 (including chain drive) was shown. This rare beast was followed by a far more conventional rendition of the same theme, the shaft-driven S800. Things were starting to look up, mechanically, but the reputation established by the S600 was still a hurdle, and the S800 wasn't much cheaper to build. Honda turned its sights to economy cars instead.

53 Bond Bug

By Name and By Nature

Perhaps the oddest car to come out of England in 1970 was the Bond Bug. Designed by Czech-born Tom Karen, it was an attempt to adapt the cheap but dowdy English three-wheeler – mostly used by invalids – into a vehicle for the hip and happening.

However, the hip and happening knew a dog when they saw it, and production lasted just four years.

All examples of the Bug (the name was at least as clever as AMC's Gremlin and just as prescient) were painted in a garish shade of orange known as tangerine, with black writing on each side to give the aura, supposedly, of a sponsored racing car.

54 Bugatti EB-110

Great Brand, Lousy Arithmetic

It seems extraordinary in light of today's 'brand is king' mentality, that one of the greatest names in automotive history could have been allowed to languish for so many years. Yet from the late 1940s until the early 1990s, the famed Bugatti brand-name and logo was seen only on a small number of old and spindly road and race cars that seemed to become more valuable with every year.

When the name came back, it was with a huge, and rather perplexing, extravagance. The man behind it was the Italian financier Romano Artioli, who bought the rights to the original logos and relaunched Bugatti with a continuation of the model designation system used by the French–Italian maestro Ettore Bugatti when he built some of the world's most capable sports and racing cars during the 1920s and 1930s.

The order of the day for the reborn brand was outrageous parties, money-no-object commemorative rallies, a *Vogue Living*-style new factory in Modena (with an air-conditioned production line), major exhibits at world motor shows, and large-format, high-gloss brochures that looked as though they cost more than some small cars.

While Artioli set about trying to prove that his new all-wheel drive EB-110 coupé (unveiled in September 1991) was a worthy claimant to the title of 'world's best supercar', many were still busy questioning where the money came from, or dividing the several million dollars spent on parties by the minuscule number of cars likely to be sold at the sort of stratospheric prices being mentioned.

The EB-110's body was low and angular, and it made extensive use of carbon-fibre. It had Lamborghini-style pop-up doors and a mid-mounted 3.5-litre V12 engine that had 60 valves and four turbochargers. The output was quoted as a massive 410 kW (545 bhp), the claimed 0-to-100 km/h time was 3.6 seconds, and trials on a banked oval produced a 'verified' top speed of 344 km/h or 206 mph. The developers claimed that 400 km/h (240 mph) would be soon achieved, but like many claims made for the new Bugatti, this one never quite bore scrutiny.

Handling was spectacularly good, but working against the Bugatti (aside from its ludicrous complexity and rushed development) was its weight, which, upward of 1,600 kg (3,520 pounds), blunted the real 0-to-100 km/h time to more like 4.5 seconds. An SS (Super Sport) version managed to cut the weight by 150 kg (330 pounds), thanks to the use of even more alloy and carbon-fibre and the deletion of all the luxury items. Publicity was gained when the Formula One star Michael Schumacher bought an EB-110 – and even more when he crashed it and blamed the inadequate brakes.

In 1993 a retro saloon, called the EB-112, was first shown. It was also four-wheel drive, but was powered by a 6-litre 12-cylinder engine. The EB-112 never made it into production. The end came in late 1994, after an estimated 154 examples of the EB-110 had been built. There were various factors: the world now had too many supercars on the market (including the McLaren F1, which was faster and generally judged to be better than the Bugatti). In addition, the world's economic bubble, which had fed the supercar boom in the first place, had well and truly burst. Anyway, the numbers needed to underpin the new Bugatti venture never really added up.

The reborn company was re-killed, but when creditors leaped in they discovered that the most valuable thing, the right to use the name and logo, was owned by a separate Artioli-controlled company and was out of their grasp. The German VW conglomerate eventually ended up with the Bugatti name (along with Bentley and others) during the great brand realignment of the mid-to-late nineties.

55 Standard Vanguard

Flagging Fast

The first Standard Vanguard represented a bold attempt to give a small post-war British car some US design razzamatazz. The boldest thing of all was that Standard's penny-pinching accountants demanded it be done without the cost of sending anyone to America. Head stylist Walter Belgrove was apparently despatched with his sketchbook to the US Embassy in London in the hope that he could sight some American iron being driven in or out. The result was the Standard Vanguard, launched in July 1947.

That US lines didn't quite work on a short British chassis is hardly a surprise. The other thing working against Standard was the name. The word 'standard' was once primarily considered in terms of the phrase: 'Setting the . . .' However, thanks to widespread use of names such as Deluxe, it came to mean 'pretty damn ordinary'. Which, in this case, was spot-on.

If the Vanguard's not-quite-to-scale US styling wasn't silly enough, its 1953 Phase II follow-up combined bits of the same silly design with a curious notchback tail that made the proportions completely different without being any less dubious. The Phase II was popularly compared with a scaled-up child's toy.

The name and the appearance of its cars weren't the only things working against the long-term survival of the brand. In 1961 Standard became a division of Leyland Motors, an English expression meaning *doomed*. The last Standard-badged car left the British factory in 1963, though assembly in Melbourne, Australia, and a few other outposts trickled into 1964. It then became a dropped Standard.

56 Messerschmitt KR

Postwar Crime

It's easy today to forget that immediately after the Second World War,
Germany (or West Germany, as the productive part was then known)
became the world's number one manufacturer of vehicles for poor
people. And when you see some of them, you realise that there is
plenty to forget.

After the war the old Autounion AG was re-formed in the Western
sector as Auto Union. Boosted by cheap German labor and well-
honed engineering skills, it became one of the world's largest
motorcycle manufacturers during the 1950s and also spat out
eccentric little two-stroke DKW delivery vans and cars. Bavaria's BMW
(Bayerische-Motoren-Werke) built something like 150,000 examples of
the horrid Isetta bubble car. Prevented from continuing with aviation
production, the famed war-plane builder Messerschmitt turned out
tiny, narrow, and equally horrid bubble cars of its own.

For Messerschmitt, the switch to car maker came about when the
company took over the Fend company's three-wheeler minicar
project. Messerschmitt, the maker of the ME-109 plane and other hits,
developed the design and, from 1953, produced a succession of
models. The first was the KR-175.

With three wheels and two seats, one behind the other, the Messie
'cabin scooter' was an almost exact blending of motor scooter and

car. It was bigger than a breadbox, but not by much, and it was certainly a great deal noisier. Regularly the subject of well-deserved ridicule, the coffin-like Messie hit the market in most countries at about half the price of a basic family saloon. It was considerably cheaper than just about anything else with more than two wheels. After Germany, it was most popular in Britain, particularly during the Suez crisis. Reasonable numbers also went to Australia and the States.

The big advantage of these minuscule vehicles (perhaps the only one) was that the alternative was invariably walking. The passenger sat with legs straddling the front seat and the maker's boast that the storage space behind the second seat could also accommodate a child seems more than a little frightening by today's standards.

The most successful model was the three-wheeler KR-200, built from 1955. Later, the more powerful (that's 'more powerful' rather than, say, 'powerful') Tiger 500 arrived.

The KR-200 initially had a two-stroke air-cooled, single-cylinder engine with a capacity of just 191 cc (11.6 cubic inches). The 'big banger' Tiger model had a half-litre engine driving twin rear wheels through a four-speed transmission. The rear wheels were positioned so closely together that it eliminated both the need for a differential and any stability advantages that might have otherwise been associated with having an extra wheel.

The Messie cabin-scooter was claimed to have many big-car features. Unfortunately, one of them was shared with the Lightburn Zeta: you needed to stop the engine and restart it to drive in reverse (that said, many examples sold in Britain didn't even have a reverse gear). On the plus side, the Messie offered full weather protection and good all-round visibility thanks to the fighter plane-style curved canopy, which was also ideal for roasting the occupants in the summer. Production ceased in Germany in 1961. By then, rising prosperity and the much more modern and practical Mini Minor had made such vehicles an anachronism.

57 Zil

Red, Square

No A to Z of bad cars can be complete without the fortuitously named Zil (although Yugoslavia's Zastava Yugo and the Ukraine's Zaz brand also do their best to fall at the rear end of the alphabet).

The Zil company commenced operations in Moscow in 1936 and for many years provided the cars of choice for Politburo members. The ludicrously large Zil 4104 and even more breathtakingly obese 41047 made it into the 21st century, each powered by a 7.7-litre V8 and weighing 3.6 and 4.2 tonnes, respectively. Although the bent-eight was ancient and fed by carburettor, the maker claimed the rather impressive power and torque figures of 232 kW (307 bhp) and 608 Nm (449 lbs/ft).

Pictured here is a 1970 model, which a Tass news agency caption called a 'light passenger car'. Although it looked like pure Americana of the 1950s, by the mid-1980s Zil models had been heavily updated – to look Dallas motorcade, 1963.

It appears that Zil production finally spluttered to a halt around 2003.

58 Bricklin SV-1

No Winged Saviour

A few years before John Z. De Lorean gave such a snappy name to sports-car failure, the Philadelphia-born Malcolm Bricklin demonstrated a similar level of automotive ineptitude with a remarkably similar car. Like the De Lorean DMC-12, the Bricklin SV-1 was an American-conceived, wedge-shaped, gullwing-doored sports car with a body built from unusual materials.

Other parallels were equally eerie: the Bricklin was produced in another country with government backing from that country, was touted as a safety innovator, had woeful build quality, and lost millions. And it didn't stop there: some backers of the Bricklin fell for the old gullwing sports-car trick a second time around and went on to put money behind De Lorean.

Malcolm Bricklin was a high-flying, fast-talking entrepreneur who started with a chain of Handyman hardware stores, then began importing motor scooters, before graduating to cars. He set up Subaru of America in 1968 but failed to make money out of it. This didn't dissuade him from trying to manufacture a car under his own name. To help the venture along, Bricklin did a deal with the Canadian province of New Brunswick, which would provide capital in return for jobs.

The Bricklin car, eventually unveiled in mid-1974, was powered by a 5.9-litre Rambler V8. The acrylic and fibreglass body was supported by a heavy-perimeter chassis claimed (without much substantiation) to greatly improve occupant protection. The slant on safety was largely because the car wasn't that quick. Anyway, a fuel crisis had struck since the car was first dreamed up, and a selfish sports car would be a hard sell. The quickly cobbled together slogan was 'The Bricklin Safety Vehicle: You'll think it's ahead of its time. We think it's about time.'

Even the gullwing doors were heralded as a safety feature because 'they opened out of the way of cyclists and pedestrians'. This was sheer nonsense, as they didn't even open out of the way of people trying to get in or out of the car. Malcolm Bricklin brashly announced that he had US$100 million worth of advance orders. But the price tag was escalating from the original projection of US$3,000 to a staggering $6,500 on release day and then on to nearly $10,000 six months later.

The Bricklin project was managed so haphazardly that the first batch of cars was shipped out of Canada incomplete. 'Finishing kits' were later sent out, but these didn't cure leaking doors or a myriad of other problems. After a few months the Rambler V8 was phased out, reputedly because bills had not been paid and the supply had been stopped, and a Ford unit was substituted.

Syndicated US motoring correspondent Gero Hoscheck conducted an early road test. 'The workmanship of the interior is quite miserable,' he reported. 'When I deposited my elbow on the armrest the whole door panel came off. I was horrified to find out the visibility was lousy. For a sports car and even by American standards the Bricklin has miserable brakes . . . Active safety also seems inadequate for evasive manoeuvres.'

In *Car and Driver* (May 1975), Don Sherman wrote 'Every [interior] furnishing seems to work against basic comfort. The roof is too low for headroom, the throttle pedal raises your right knee into interference with the leather steering-wheel rim and the lumpy seat doesn't offer support for your thighs. And it's a hard car to see out of as well.'

It was hardly a surprise when, in October 1975, the gates to the Bricklin plants in East Saint John and Minto were locked. Malcolm B was now saying he needed another Can$20 million to $25 million to keep the venture afloat. Not even New Brunswick officials (who had now spent Can$23 million, or five times the amount originally agreed) were that silly this time around.

Bricklin had originally said that his company would build 10,000 cars in the first year, that the number would rise to 50,000 by 1978. He also boasted that he had huge banks of advance orders. In reality, only 2,900 cars were built, and more than a third of them were unsold when the company shut its doors for good.

59 Toyota Publica 700

Tiny Tin

The Publica – the name perhaps deriving from the Latin for 'flimsy and odious' – was a finned, two-door saloon with styling that pre-empted that of the Trabant, a vehicle with styling that didn't need pre-empting.

Even back in the early 1960s some windscreen-wiper motors had more kick than the Publica's 700-cc twin-cylinder air-cooled screecher, arguably the worst single piece of mechanical equipment to come out of Japan's largest car maker.

Trying to keep up with the traffic was a problem because, by the time the Publica had built up a decent head of steam, most of the traffic had already arrived where it was going. When fitted with the optional two-speed automatic transmission, the Publica took 53 seconds to accelerate from rest to 100 km/h (62.5 mph). A modern family saloon takes about 8 seconds.

However, Toyota's adventure with miniature cars was almost over. In 1966 the company assumed a controlling interesting in Daihatsu and delegated to that company the job of producing tiny, underpowered, screaming little horrors.

60 Ford Capri

Open Season

It should have been so good. It brought together proven Mazda mechanical components, a swag of top designers, highly skilled engineers, and the promise of the first affordable convertible sports car since the MGB died of old age and neglect in 1980. Yes, it should have been a Mazda MX-5. Alas, it was only a Ford Capri.

The Capri in question – styled in Italy, fitted with Japanese mechanical components and screwed together in Australia specifically for the American market – is not to be confused with Britain's Ford Capri, that archetypal Essex girl and Barrow Boy conveyance (about which the least said the better). Nor indeed with the US's earlier Mercury Capri, which had entirely different reasons to be disliked.

Where to begin with this one? Back in the 1980s Mazda and its partial parent, Ford, were simultaneously working on small four-cylinder roadsters. Although it was obvious to all that Mazda's Japanese-built MX-5 would have the edge in styling and superior handling, insiders didn't see it as serious competition for Ford. Ford would have its roadster out first and the Capri had one thing that Mazda had no answer for. Information on exactly what this one thing was has since been lost, but we do know that Ford pushed ahead, even though there were so many delays that Mazda beat it to the market and signed up most of the potential customers for a light convertible sports car.

Furthermore, the Ford Motor Company decided to use the little roadster as bait to get younger punters into its funereal Lincoln-Mercury dealerships. Ford Australia's main chance was merely the American Ford company's novel experiment. Which failed.

Not that everything could be blamed on the recipients. The Capri was underdeveloped, rather lacking in the quality department, and hard to get excited about. And the styling was questionable. The tail-lights looked like they were stuck on upside down, the interior was pure budget hatchback, and the slab-sided wedge body was more 1970s than 1990s. It was front-wheel drive too, something that roadster aficionados viewed with suspicion.

People will forgive a sports car many sins if it's pretty. If not, it's got to be very quick. Here Ford missed out again. Even in its turbo form, the Capri felt less sporty than its Mazda competitor, and Ford's two-plus-two seat configuration (versus Mazda's two seats only) and

bigger boot were not enough to make the difference. With the MX-5, lowering the roof was a simple chuck over the shoulder. With the Capri, you almost needed to call for roadside assistance. Then there was the scuttle shake, plus a generous selection of rattles, squeaks, leaks, and design failures.

A review by the US's *Consumer Reports* didn't help. The magazine was unimpressed with the flimsy body structure, the poor assembly ('the exterior finish was atrocious'), the poor driving position, low occupant comfort, poor switchgear, the feeling that it was a parts bin special ('many different pieces that aren't connected well'), the leaking convertible top and much more. But considering the type of vehicle it was, the killer blow was the conclusion that 'a sports car should be fun to drive – and our test drivers all agree that the Capri isn't.'

Some Capri problems were fixed with the Series II. But it was too late. By being pretty and having its act together from day one, the MX-5 sold strongly and scooped just about every 'car of the year' award around the world. At one stage it seemed people were inventing awards just to give them to the Mazda MX-5. By contrast, Ford Australia struggled from day one. The company needed sales of 25,000 cars a year to make its Capri project viable. The figure was almost reached in the first year, with nearly 20,000 sales in the States and 4,000 in Australia. After that, the Capri didn't come close.

To help with the numbers, Ford Australia tried to launch the Capri in the EC. This plan was thwarted by Ford of Europe, which feared it would steal sales from local models. As anyone who has driven a Capri would attest, that was extremely unlikely.

61 Sabra Sports

Spiked!

It was going to be Israel's big automotive break. It was going to be a dashing two-seater roadster made in Haifa. It was going to be exported to the US in big numbers. As it turned out, it wasn't, it wasn't and it wasn't.

The company behind the project, Autocars Co. Ltd, had already achieved modest success building versions of British Reliant three- and four-wheelers for the Israeli market. It had even garnered some US interest when it displayed vehicles at the 1960 New York Trade Fair.

With an appetite for US action whetted, the company's managing director, Itzhak Shubinksy, spotted a vehicle he thought gave the best possible chance of making an impact. It was the UK-built, fibreglass-bodied Ashley GT, and Shubinksy snapped up the rights, renamed it after a cactus, and contracted Reliant to hurriedly re-engineer it for the US. Unfortunately, in the rush Reliant misheard Shubinksy and *horridly* re-engineered it.

Furthermore, the Autocars factory wasn't ready, so the Sabra Sports was made in the UK by Reliant and shipped directly to the US. Despite all the fuss, the plastic-bodied car with the strangely squared rear wheel-arches (and even stranger front bumper overriders), sold just 150 units in America, and within a remarkably short time the Israeli

sports car project was cactus. Reliant tried to salvage some of its investment by reworking the car and launching it in the UK as the Sabre, while Autocars went back to the boring utilitarian models that were its normal fare.

62 Jaguar XJ220

The Fattest Cat

In the late 1980s a vast number of people seemed to be in possession of a vast quantity of money. And by a quirk of financial history, this new wealth – apparently created out of nothing – had been distributed in perfectly inverse proportion to taste and restraint.

What better opportunity to launch the widest, ugliest, most ostentatious, altogether stupidest Jaguar of all time?

From the moment this car – known as the XJ220 – was shown in 1988, things went slightly potty. The geeks paid homage by starting work on the first ever computer game based around a single car (it came out in 1989 for Commodore Amiga and Atari ST), while potential buyers hammered on the showroom doors trying to get their hands on the real thing. Never mind that the XJ220 was going to cost £415,554 ex-factory, was so wide it wouldn't fit down many roads, so powerful it was totally impractical in traffic, and so highly strung it would need to be shipped back to headquarters for obscenely expensive, racing car-style servicing at regular intervals. Within forty-eight hours of the announcement of 'limited edition' production, 1,500 people had put up their hands for the 350 cars scheduled to be built.

These people either believed they needed one (they didn't) or that it would go up in value (it wouldn't). Those who got in first paid a 10 per cent deposit, while others forked out even more to buy someone else's spot in the queue. Behind this daft scenario, which was all to end in tears, there was a fair bit of cutting, chopping, and changing within the Coventry cathouse.

The original show car had featured a 6.2-litre V12 and all-wheel drive. By the time specifications of the production version had been fixed, the XJ220 had a 3.5-litre V6 (a later iteration of the engine fitted to the Metro 6R4 Rally car years before), and this powered only the rear wheels. Nonetheless, the production version boasted power and torque figures of 404 kW (537 bhp) and 642 Nm (474 lbs/ft), plus the ability to rocket from rest to 60 mph [97 km/h] in under four seconds and to 100 mph [161 km/h] in under eight seconds.

The XJ name was designed to bring to mind the XK120 model and the stillborn XJ13 racer. The '220' was the projected top speed in miles per hour [equating to 354 km/h], which would make the XJ220 the world's fastest production car. Except the real top speed came up at least 7 mph short – and the later, greater (but equally unsuccessful) McLaren F1 was soon to blow the Jaguar and other 'world's fastest car' aspirants into the weeds.

The XJ220 was 2.22 metres (7.3 feet) wide, a fraction under 5 metres (16.5 feet) long, and weighed 1,470 kg (3,234 pounds). Each of the four tyres was unique (so there was no spare), and each tyre cost about the same as a secondhand car. At the press launch a journalist from the *Guardian* grabbed the wrong gear at high speed and, depending on whose report you believe, did thousands, or tens of thousands' worth of damage. He wasn't the only one who had difficulty controlling this fearsomely quick, cumbersome, and harsh machine.

Autocar magazine said the engine sounded like 'a pail of nuts and bolts being poured through a Magimix'. In short, the XJ220 was not the sort of thing the fashion designers and rock stars in the queue were even slightly likely to enjoy driving. Worse still, the production run didn't begin until July 1992, by which stage the economy had turned, the McLaren F1 had been unveiled, and so many buyers were so keen not to proceed they were willing to walk away from their substantial deposits. That wasn't good enough for Jaguar, which called in the lawyers to force completion. Many prospective buyers had already gone broke in the downturn, or simply refused to supply the balance, citing such things as the changed mechanical specifications. Settlements were reached, but it was a miserable business all around.

And how collectable was this so-called instant classic? A dozen or so years after the launch, a pristine example with low miles would struggle to fetch a quarter of the original price. And did anyone feel sorry for the fools who had bought them new? Not bloody likely.

63 Fiat ESV 1500

Soft Sell

ESV was a buzz word of 1970. Not that it was a word, as such. It was an acronym for Experimental Safety Vehicle, and came about because in that year the USA's Department of Transportation responded to the new safety lobby by coining the term, publishing a series of ESV guidelines and recommending that car makers set to work on them if they wanted to sell cars in the USA in the future.

The general rules seemed to be these: get an undistinguished car, restyle it to make it even uglier, cover all the sharp bits inside and out with thick padding, then devise a system of interior safety webs, belts, buckles and harnesses more complex than the wiring diagram of the London Underground.

Most ESVs made you grateful that looks can't kill. This Fiat effort was at least as silly as most, being unsightly enough to be unsaleable, impossibly heavy and too expensive to mass-produce. Mind you, being a Fiat of the 1970s, its main safety feature would have been that it spent most of its time off the road being repaired.

64 Chevrolet Corvair

The Roll Model

In the 1965 book *Unsafe at Any Speed*, Ralph Nader, a Harvard Law School graduate, set out to paint General Motors as a corporation with a greater interest in profits than in the safety of its customers. There was no better illustration, Nader asserted, than the rear-engined Chevrolet Corvair, which, he said, had a flawed, penny-pinching suspension system that caused drivers to lose control during turns and flip the car over.

GM responded in what it considered a sensible, practical, and reasonable way. It hired private detectives to follow Nader in the hope of proving he was homosexual.

But why did GM produce a car as unlikely as the Corvair in the first place? It was a response to the success of the VW Beetle in the US during the 1950s. This convinced Chevrolet it needed a lighter car in its armoury and if an air-cooled, horizontally opposed engine in the tail could work for the Germans, why not for the Americans?

Being Chevrolet, it was decided that bigger was better, even if the Corvair was originally envisaged as a light car. So it ended up with a six-cylinder engine in the tail, albeit with a comparatively modest capacity (for the States) of 140 cubic inches, or 2.3 litres. As well as being larger than the Beetle, the Corvair was a great deal more modern, with a monocoque body (in which the body is integral with the chassis), and aluminium engine. From a company better known for tarting up old designs with new bodywork than re-engineering from the ground up, this was extraordinary stuff.

The first Corvair, released in late 1959, broke other Detroit trends with an austere interior, and bodywork unadorned with fins or fields of chrome. It was offered as a two- or four-door. A van, station wagon, and curious 'Rampside pickup' soon followed, then a convertible and a pioneering turbocharged engine option also appeared.

Nader's allegations concentrated on these early Corvairs of 1960 to 1963, which he described as 'the one-car accident'. The Corvair certainly had a tendency to oversteer, or hang its tail out. Enthusiasts loved this, but it was not ideal for those who didn't adjust their driving style (most American cars tended to plough forward into a corner with huge understeer), or were lax about maintaining correct tyre pressures.

By the time Nader attacked, there were 103 Corvair lawsuits against GM, and Chevrolet had modified the suspension to control the rear 'tuck in' that *Unsafe at Any Speed* blamed for unpredictable handling. But the Ford Mustang was released in 1964 and did more to kill the Corvair than Nader ever could. It offered a powerful V8, and with fuel being so cheap, who cared about the Corvair's greater fuel economy or mechanical sophistication?

A svelte new Corvair body for 1965 was not enough to tackle Mustang, while the notorious (and bungled) Nader surveillance operation failed to rid GM of its 'consumer advocate' problem. GM's president, James Roche, was forced to apologise to Nader before a Senate subcommittee, and the company eventually handed over

US$425,000 for invasion of privacy. (It wasn't only homosexuality GM was looking for; evidence tendered showed it would have been equally happy to prove Nader was a Communist or secret beneficiary of Corvair lawsuits.)

Like any good zealot, Nader used his newfound wealth to dig even deeper into the automotive industry – and the meat industry and almost every other potential infringer of consumer rights. In 1966, as a direct result of the Corvair affair, the US federal government announced its first National Traffic and Motor Vehicle Safety Act.

It is widely believed Chevrolet would have dropped the Corvair in 1967 for commercial reasons, but didn't want to be seen to be running. So the Corvair stumbled on until 1969, recording sales of just 6,000 in its final year, compared with nearly 330,000 in 1961. Buyers of the last examples needed to be coaxed with a credit towards the purchase of a future Chevrolet.

Meanwhile, none of the eight Corvair cases that went to trial were successful for the plaintiffs, and the final twist came in 1972, when the National Highway and Traffic Safety Administration finally released its report into Nader's allegations. It concluded: 'The handling and stability performance of the 1960–63 Corvair does not result in an abnormal potential for loss of control or rollover, and it is at least as good as the performance of some contemporary vehicles, both foreign and domestic.'

Nader considered the report a whitewash. Corvair supporters had the bittersweet comfort of knowing the car had been pardoned after its execution.

65 Ligier

Nosy Parker

It was built by one-time Formula One racing-car constructor Ligier, but this little French box on wheels had only one motor sport connection: it was the pits.

Due to an almost inexplicable loophole in French road laws that existed until the early 1990s, a vehicle with an engine capacity of less than 125 cc, or an output of less than 4 kW (5.3 bhp), did not need to be registered, nor did the person behind the wheel need to hold a driving licence. This led to the development of a type of little car the French derisively referred to as a *pot du yaourt* (pot of yogurt). The *PdY* found immediate favour with very old and very young drivers, while rental companies bulk-purchased them to offer to people whose licences had been suspended for drink-driving. Ligier was just one of several companies happy to supply.

Weaving in and out of manic Parisian traffic, these tubs of curdled milk were not governed by noise or pollution laws and their engines (usually two-stroke petrol engines, sometimes diesel and very occasionally electric) tended to spit out palls of dark smoke as they clackchuttered along. And, in accordance with French automotive custom, when *PdY*s were parked it was invariably on pedestrian crossings, across footpaths or on top of motorcyclists. Since they carried no registration plates or labels of identification, the owners couldn't be brought to account by police, though the vehicles themselves were often lifted and moved, or even capsized by aggrieved *citoyens*.

Despite tougher regulations, including the requirement that they be registered and carry number plates, the *PdY*s still haven't been completely stamped out.

66 Austin Allegro

A Streetcar Named Dire

The early 1970s were perhaps the greyest time of all for British industry, with the three-day week, petrol rationing, power cuts, endless strikes, rampant inflation and widespread discontent on every level. And no car better reflects all that greyness and misery than the Austin Allegro.

Announced in May 1973 as British Leyland's 'high-technology' weapon to increase small car sales at home and abroad, the Allegro managed to do neither and annoyed so many owners with its vile reliability that it was widely known as the 'All Aggro'.

The Allegro replaced the 1100/1300 series, a widely applauded BMC design from Alec Issigonis, father of the Mini. That car had been adventurous; this one was anything but and VW was about the change the small car world with the Golf hatchback. BMC/Leyland, of course, had already built hatchbacks

and the shape of the Allegro suggests it was first thought of with a lift-up rear door. Yet some nong in management decided it should have a conventional boot so it didn't kill sales of the Austin Maxi (that job was left to the Golf).

Therefore, the Allegro turned out to be a standard saloon, and a dumpy one at that. The stunted tail led to the story that when the Allegro was turned backwards during wind tunnel development the aerodynamic figures improved. In reality, it is unlikely the bloated little Allegro was ever in the same postal district as a wind tunnel.

As with its predecessor, the Allegro was front-wheel drive. Two and four-door models were available with variations on familiar engines (the A-Series in the smaller capacity models, the E-Series in the 1.5- and 1.75-litre versions) and the usual collection of mechanical components from the Leyland parts bin. The ambitions were enormous. 'It is our song for Europe,' boasted managing director George Turnbull, who claimed the Allegro would appeal to buyers from the Arctic Circle to 'the toe of Italy' because of its leading technology and the way 'the eye is beguiled by its excellent proportions'.

The thing that attracted the most attention was the square steering wheel. Exhibiting more effort and imagination than they had put into the car, Leyland bosses dubbed this the 'Quartic logical steering device'. Many believed the stated advantages (better view of the instruments, more leverage during parking) were after-the-fact justifications and the wheel was that way because designers hadn't left enough room between the standard wheel and the driver's seat.

The new Hydragas suspension was similar to the sophisticated and smooth-riding system fitted to Citroëns – in that it was complex and unreliable. Other similarities were hard to find. The Allegro's structural rigidity was so poor that glass panels tended to pop out, rear wheels flew off due to bearing problems and water leaks could be so prolific that occupants and their cargo were thoroughly drenched. Stupid little design flaws were legion; the seatbelt reels for the front seats, for example, were placed exactly in the way of anyone trying to slide their feet into the rear.

Despite all this, the Allegro was adopted by the British police. It was a move that no doubt boosted the confidence of criminals across the nation. One change made by the force though was to replace all the Quartic steering wheels with old-fashioned Roundic ones. Leyland made the same change across all Allegros when the Series 2 was announced in 1975. A three-door estate version was launched at the same time. The Allegro Series 3 arrived in 1979, but probably should have stayed at home. And did we mention the ridiculous Vanden Plas 1500 version, a so-called luxury version with leather and walnut trim and an upright grille?

Although undercooked on day one, the Allegro lasted ten years and Leyland engineers had to spend most of them furiously trying to iron out the bugs. Yet bizarrely, some people are trying to recast the Allegro as a cult classic, including a Birmingham vicar, Reverend Colin Corke. He has owned more than fifty Allegros, and has spent a claimed £12,000 restoring a rare 1750SS model. He seems to have missed the point that the 1750SS is rare for a good reason: not many people bought them when they were new, they quickly fell apart, and no one else has thought it worth putting them back together.

67 Subaru 360

The Sub-Veedub

The late 1950s and early 1960s brought a flood of Japanese microcars, including the Mazda 360, the Suzulight 360, and the Mitsubishi 500. Each provides a reminder that before Japan made cars that were reliable, well-built, and stylish, they made cars that were un, badly, and less than.

The forerunner of these minis, though, was the Subaru 360, created when someone at Fuji Heavy Industries discovered that Japan's 'micro-vehicle' legislation – created to make motorcycles and three-wheeled delivery vans affordable – could be adapted for cars. The 360 appeared in March 1958, sneakily complying by having an overall length less than 3 metres (9.9 feet, which was shorter than the original Mini Minor), a weight below 350 kg (771 pounds), and a sub-360-cc (22-cubic-inch) engine. Buyers could use a cheaper restricted driving licence and pay about one-tenth the road tax of those buying a full-sized vehicle.

The Subaru 360 was designed to be just big enough to carry a family of four while offering all-weather protection. Instrumentation consisted solely of a speedometer, the turn signals were manually operated and the four-speed transmission lacked proper synchromesh. The doors were of the forward-opening 'suicide' type and the body a mishmash of poorly fitting panels. The bottom of the rear wheels tucked in under the tail to make sure the finished product never looked quite secure in the upright position. But the 360 was cheap.

Many considered the Subaru a shrunken VW Beetle. They certainly had in common an air-cooled, rear-mounted engine, rack-and-pinion steering and fully independent suspension using torsion bars on all wheels. However, the Subaru had only two cylinders and its microscopic engine – a two-stroke with a built-in propensity for

overheating and seizing – screamed its head off to produce just 11.5 kW (16 bhp). Although the maximum speed was claimed as 80 km/h (50 mph), the handling was so dodgy it is unlikely anyone was game enough to try it. And with 25.4 cm (10-inch) wheels (the Subaru 'scooped' the Mini Minor on its least commendable feature), the 360 could disappear into things that larger vehicles didn't even consider to be potholes.

FHI used the name Subaru (rather than Rabbit, the name of its scooters), taking it from the Japanese term for a cluster of six stars that form part of the Taurus constellation. It managed to build just 604 vehicles in the first year, but convertible and light-commercial derivatives joined the line-up as production improved. Subaru also offered a 423-cc (26-cubic-inch) engine in export markets.

In the United States the paths of Subaru and entrepreneur Malcolm Bricklin crossed in the late sixties in a fashion as colourful as one would expect from the man who would later give his name to one of the world's truly incompetent sports cars. Bricklin formed Subaru of America and marketed the Subaru 360 sedan under the unlikely slogan 'Cheap and ugly does it'.

By US standards, the Subaru 360 was so small it should have been labelled 'Not for individual sale'. Yet the car's tininess exempted it from emission and safety regulations. It was a much-needed exemption.

The timing was interesting, for if you were to create a list of everything that Americans were looking for in a car in 1968, the Subaru would have lined up perfectly with the 'not required' column. To Americans the VW was already minuscule – a smaller scale replica of it made no sense at all. *Road & Track* magazine stated that the Subaru was 'of uncommon ugliness' before recording a dismally slow 0-to-50 mph (0-to-80 km/h) acceleration time of 36 seconds (the road testers were aiming for 60 mph (96.5 km/h), but the car wouldn't make it). Bricklin made a song and dance of the frugal fuel use, but that was an advantage almost anywhere but the US, where fuel was so cheap that Oldsmobile and others happily marketed cars with engines twenty times the size of the Subaru's.

The American lack of interest in the 360 became even more pronounced when *Consumer Reports* magazine labelled it 'the most unsafe car in America'. With Subaru's six stars in freefall and 1,000 unsold cars in stock, Bricklin started FasTrack International, a franchise operation offering dollar-per-lap car-racing theme parks. Each franchise came with ten Subaru 360s, presumably to remind budding racing drivers that motor sport is dangerous. When FasTrack achieved all the success it deserved, Bricklin slid out of the whole operation and embarked on the path to losing millions of other people's dollars building a sports car bearing his own name.

Meanwhile, for all its faults, the little Subaru stayed in production until 1970. By then, one million had been sold, mostly in Japan.

68 Daihatsu Bee

No Honey

From the early 1950s,
Japan's Daihatsu
repeatedly attempted to
make a passenger car out
of one of its three-wheeled
delivery trucks. The result
finally came to market in
1958 after several false
starts. It was styled with a
side profile which made it

look like a conventional saloon car, in the hope no one
would notice it was missing a front wheel. To further confuse the
enemy, it had a long bonnet, despite the engine being in the tail.

Even when its styling was put to one side, where it belonged, the
Bee was not the knees. It was crude in construction, woefully
underpowered (production versions had a dubious 540-cc air-cooled
engine which struggled to drag along the new bodywork) and not
altogether stable. Sales were infinitesimal. It was a decade or so
before the company built its first four-wheeled passenger car and
many more years further on before it produced anything you'd feel
even slightly safe sitting in.

69 Hillman Imp

Frailty, Thy Name Is Hillman

The car was called Imp and every second advertisement and newspaper article used words such as IMPressive and IMPortant. Closer to the mark, however, was IMPrudent. Because although the Imp was British small car innovation at its most venturesome, it was also financial suicide.

The whole sorry saga started in the mid-1950s, when the Rootes Group (known for its solid Hillman and Humber models) started talking about a small-car project. This was a surprise as its directors had earlier made it clear they had little interest in economy models, and were among those who had so famously turned down the Volkswagen company after the war.

The talk continued to be just that until the success of the Mini Minor. At that point Rootes' directors decided an all-new small car was their single greatest priority. In a breathless three-year period, the design of a radical Hillman small car was finalised and an all-new plant was built in Scotland to manufacture it.

In May 1963 the car hit the market amid enormous excitement. The Imp seemed as radical as the Mini, and was equally sporting. And while the Mini was front-engined, front-wheel drive, the Imp was the complete opposite. Furthermore, it featured such things as a motor sport-derived all-aluminium engine and a hatchback-style lift-up rear window. In the UK, 20,000 orders were taken in the two days following the Imp's unveiling. And when the car was launched in other markets soon afterwards, buyers seemed equally taken with the newest Hillman.

Alas, the exciting promise of those early days quickly faded. As the Imp demonstrated more than its share of teething problems and design limitations, the Mini's success seemed to grow and grow, casting a huge shadow that all but obscured the littlest Hillman.

The dictionary defines an imp as a little devil or demon, or a mischievous child. Hillman's version lived up to its name, ungratefully helping to bankrupt its creators. (In 1964 the haemorrhaging Rootes Group was snapped up by the Chrysler Corporation.)

Technically, the Imp was nothing if not interesting. The body was a fraction bigger than the Mini's, while its 875-cc engine was produced in collaboration with Coventry Climax (the company that had produced world-beating Cooper and Lotus racing engines). This powerplant was laid over at a 45-degree angle, lowering the centre of gravity and making room for a modest luggage compartment above.

The Imp had sharp handling (though with an inelegant tendency to cock its front wheels in the air at speed), a nice gear-shift and effective brakes. However, the recommended tyre pressures (15 psi/103 kPa in the front, 30psi/206 kPa in the rear) gave some idea that it wasn't a car with perfect, 50–50 weight distribution. There were other gripes: the Imp was initially available only in drab colours and lacked front flipper windows (then considered a necessity). It was also noisy and unduly susceptible to side winds. Quality was a lucky dip. The Scots building it were mainly new to the car industry and the design was

undercooked anyway. Many Imps demonstrated a voracious hunger for throttle cables, water pumps and other things not generally regarded as 'consumables'. The engine's tendency to overheat and warp became legendary.

The quality story became even worse as the 1960s progressed. Sales continued to fall and the bean counters battled the situation by cutting costs rather than improving the vehicle. Nonetheless, the Imp stumbled on until 1976. Two years later Hillman – a brand dating to before the First World War – joined the enormously long list of famous British car marques to fall from the sky. Once again, pilot error seemed solely responsible.

70 Honda Z

Scream de la Scream

Anyone who took even a brief look at the minuscule Honda Z would be hard pressed to believe the company that built it would one day be a dominant force in motor sport, and a respected maker of large luxury cars and mid-engined supercars.

Indeed, the casual observer might very well have laughed out loud and taken a bet on how quickly the Z would join such other Japanese automotive failures as the Cony Guppy, Paddle PD33 and Flying Feather. There was, after all, something frankly ridiculous about the Honda's combination of zany curves, upswept waistline, television screen rear window, sports-car interior, lawn-mower-sized engine and incongruous go-fast stripes.

Launched in the UK in early 1972 at £719 (making it dearer than the basic Mini or Hillman Imp), the Z was available only with bright orange exterior paint. Despite the sports-car pretensions, it was under 3 metres (10 feet) long, only 1.3 metres (4¼ feet) wide and powered by a tiny two-cylinder engine.

The Z was based on the mechanical components of the Honda Scamp (also known as the N360), a sort of Japanese Mini Minor first exported in the late 1960s. The Scamp set new benchmarks for noisiness, yet had surprised people with the performance it produced from an engine less than half the size of the Mini unit (the Scamp had just 356-cc up its mechanical sleeve). As with the Scamp, the Z package owed its existence to the Japanese domestic tax regime, which allowed special concessions to sub-360-cc, sub-3-metre microcars. The British market, however, was lucky enough to receive a 'big-banger' 600-cc engine instead of the standard 360-cc screamer.

The press used such oh-so-1970s terms as 'the most way-out micro yet', while *Motor* noted that the Z caused nearly as much interest as a Lamborghini Espada it had recently tested, 'although with due respect to Honda it was probably for a different reason'.

That Honda itself had yet to master hyperbole was shown by a brochure which boasted a 'quite spacious interior' and 'quite enough power to assure adequate speeds'. There was also the cautious 'If you consider it carefully, you're quite likely to find this Honda can fill your motoring needs most adequately.'

The Z weighed little more than half a tonne. The shrieking two-cylinder 360-cc engine revved to nearly 10,000 rpm and cranked out 23 kW (not bad from a third of a litre, but not much with four aboard), while the 600-cc developed just three-quarters of a kilowatt (1 bhp) more but was slightly less cacophonous. Either way, if you could stand the noise and didn't overload it, the Z could zip comfortably along with the traffic, reaching speeds of up to 112 km/h (70 mph) in 600-cc guise. But it took its time to get there. The standing quarter mile required about 24 seconds but you still had to wait another 8 seconds or so to reach 97 km/h (60 mph).

The early Zs had air-cooling but a water-cooled, twin-carburettor engine was later introduced. Equipment levels were high, though the quality and reliability combo that would eventually make Japanese cars so successful was still far from a standard inclusion. Many Honda Zs tended to rattle their panels loose and even unglued their back windows. And when mechanical wear reared its ugly head, the cost of fixing the relatively complex powerplant often outstripped the value of the car (the Lilliputian engine case also contained the gearbox and differential).

The Z quickly became the most successful Honda four-wheeler ever exported. This was a minor achievement if you look at its oddball forebears, but it was nonetheless the start of bigger and better things. In 1973 Honda started exporting the Civic and intensified its drive to become more sophisticated and mainstream. The company suddenly seemed embarrassed by the cheerfully goofy image presented by the Z, and sales stopped soon afterwards.

71 Ssangyong Korando

Ignore Me Not

There were many stupid things about the Korando, but perhaps the most dippy of all was the name. Korando isn't a majestic beast, a celestial body, the name of an egotistical automotive magnate or any of the things after which people usually name cars. It is a corruption of 'Korea can do'. And that's despite the fact that one look at this crimped-nose Jeep makes it immediately obvious that if there is one thing Korea can do, it's not this.

For many years Ssangyong built military Jeeps under licence on behalf of the South Korean government. The Korando was an attempt to adapt such a vehicle for private use by restyling it, powering it with a Korean-built version of a pensioned-off Mercedes-Benz six-cylinder engine and throwing in every luxury feature on hand.

English designer Ken Greenley penned the lines under contract, and he – perhaps uniquely – argued it was a success. Greenley's reasoning was that the styling made people stand up and take notice. 'If you do stuff that people don't even talk about and have no comment on and no interest at all, this means you must have failed somewhere along the line,' he argued in the press. 'To be ignored completely, is . . . I mean, that's awful.'

Korando isn't the only naff composite badge to come out of Korea. Kia's Carens takes its handle from a combination of 'car' and 'Renaissance', while Retona means, wait for it, 'return to nature'. The name of the Sportage wagon denotes – you guessed it – 'sport' and 'portage'.

And just how successful was the boldly styled Korando in establishing Ssangyong as a distinct and successful brand? Shortly after the model's launch, the company was absorbed into Daewoo, which was already wilting fast and would soon collapse three-quarters dead into the arms of General Motors. The answer, then, would appear to be 'not very'.

72 Nissan Pintara

A Bird? A Plane? No, Alas, a Superhatch

It was a decade that produced its fair share of Australian motoring horrors, but one car bestrode the harbour of 1980s failures like a colossus. It is the 1989 Nissan Pintara, which managed to be every bit as unsuccessful as the Leyland P76 without being even a tiny fraction as interesting. Indeed, when the Pintara petered out in an excruciatingly expensive meltdown of jobs, dollars, and egos, nobody even hinted that they were about to start an enthusiasts' club.

Where to start? During the 1980s Nissan Australia went berserk with its corporate chequebook, spending something like Aus$500 million upgrading its Clayton, Victoria, plant with the stated aim of producing 100,000 cars per year. What the company was going to do with all those cars was another question, but either no one asked it, or someone came up with a very persuasive way of saying it would all be right on the night.

Nissan Australia's then managing director was Ivan Deveson, something of a self-styled Lido 'Lee' Iacocca (the extroverted Ford, then Chrysler, boss who wrote two large books – both about himself). With thumbs hooked into his trademark red braces, Deveson described the new-generation Pintara as 'Australian-designed' and boasted that it would be a big seller for the local arms of Nissan and Ford (which would have its own Corsair version), and would be

exported to places such as Japan 'in large numbers'. Wrong, wrong, wrong and wrong.

The problems started as soon as the Pintara was unveiled. It turned out to be merely a revamp of an already tired Japanese market front-drive 'Bluebird' saloon. A locally adapted Pintara variant called Superhatch didn't help. More a hunchback than a hatchback, it was as clumsy as the saloon was dull. It couldn't leap tall buildings and the speed of its sales brought to mind not so much a speeding bullet as a spent cartridge.

Scan the sales figures for the whole Pintara family: in 1990 just 13,688 Pintaras were sold (Mitsubishi Australia's Magna, which cleared more than twice as many was considered to be struggling). In 1991 the Pintara body count was 11,819, then, in 1992, just 5,569. And Nissan dealers had to 'guts' (heavily discount) just about every one of them to achieve even these unimpressive figures. Ford did worse with its Corsair twin, selling 7,632, 3,562, and 1,891 cars during the same years.

It should be noted, however, that there have been plenty of cars worse than the Pintara – several of them made by Nissan. The Pintara was fairly well screwed together and had acceptable equipment levels, and even the bottom-spec 2-litre version offered reasonable performance. But there wasn't a single compelling reason to choose one above the competition. And to achieve anything like its lofty ambitions, Nissan Australia needed more than a Superhatch. It needed a miracle machine.

By the end of 1992, local production of the Pintara/Corsair was finally killed off, and Nissan admitted to losses of hundreds of millions of dollars. And those high-volume Japanese exports? Only 1,000 or so were shipped, each with a stuffed koala in the glove compartment and a badge saying 'Nissan Aussie'. The humiliation was complete.

73 Oldsmobile Toronado

Trailing from the Front

It was heralded in 1966 as 'America's car of the year' by no lesser authority than *Motor Trend*, which also raved about its handling. Others also gushed profusely, calling it the most desirable Oldsmobile of all time.

Maybe there was something in the air (it was the 1960s). Maybe aficionados of the brand were just over-excited about the first new mainstream front-drive US car since the Cord of the 1930s. But exactly what the cheer squad was thinking is hard to say, because to love the Toronado generally involved falling head over heels with the body – which many did, despite its wallowing tail and front guards designed to neatly slice pedestrians in two – and ignoring almost everything else.

The Toronado was claimed to be the largest front-wheel drive car ever, a very curious achievement. The main advantage of powering the front rather than the rear wheels is to improve packaging efficiency. Sure, the cabin floor of the Toronado was flat because there was no driveshaft running fore to aft, but considering the limousine-like 5.36-metre (17½-feet) overall length, the interior should have been about the size of an Imperial ballroom.

Alas, much of the potential passenger room was lost in those huge overhangs, while a stunted two-door cabin with sloping roofline squandered a great deal of what was left. The rear seat occupants put up with leg room crampingly similar to that of another front-wheel drive car, the Mini Minor, while the driver endured two massive blind spots due to those mighty rear pillars. As for harnessing front-drive's weight advantages, the Toronado tipped the scales at only a tiny shade under 2 tonnes.

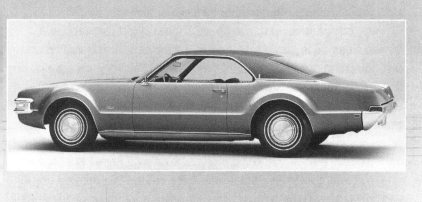

Like the Cord, the Toronado had its headlights secreted behind covers. There were strange 'power bulges' over the wheel arches. 'Toronado is all man – right down to that man sized trunk', cried one ad. What it didn't mention is that even men who were all men objected to the ridiculous weight of the massive doors and within a year or so of the car's release the company had to introduce a 'built-in assist' mechanism to help open and close them.

After congratulating the buyer on choosing the Toronado, the owner's manual remarked 'never has there been a car with so many distinguishing characteristics'. One of these characteristics was high temperatures under that massive bonnet, which led to a spate of engine fires. Another was diabolical handling. If the Toronado had great road manners (as suggested by the US press), then it was only when compared with other Oldsmobiles. With such bulk over the front wheels, the Toronado did more than chew up tyres at a fearsome rate. It lifted understeer – the tendency to plough forward in a corner – to a new art. And with such a vast engine and larduous kerb weight, what did engineers use to stop the Toronado? Feeble drum brakes all round.

The bonnet that went on for ever housed a gargantuan 7-litre (425-cubic-inch) V8. This fed its power to the front wheels via a complex split transmission system with the three-speed auto box under the left cylinder bank and a torque converter mounted on the back of the engine. The two were connected by a chain and sprocket. The system was reputedly based on a patent purchased from Ford – which couldn't make it work. And because Oldsmobile buyers ultimately didn't care which wheels were being driven, and the Toronado took no other advantage of its chosen mechanical configuration, all the expense and complexity was for nothing.

Fuel consumption was everything you'd expect with a 7-litre engine driving through a slushy three-speed auto. Despite this, more than 40,000 Toronados were sold in the first year, and a few were exported. Australia's *Sports Car World* magazine described the wet-weather handling as lousy and the braking as diabolical. In the UK in 1967, the Toronado was priced at exactly £1,000 more than a Jensen Interceptor, itself famous for being ludicrously expensive (but nonetheless shown by *Motor* to be faster, better accelerating and more fuel efficient than the Oldsmobile).

When US sales dropped by about half in year two, Oldsmobile invoked the time-honoured car-makers' solution: when in trouble, increase the engine size and add more chrome. For 1968, Toronados were fitted with 7.4-litre engines.

For the 1969 model year, front discs became standard, lifting the Toronado's braking performance so dramatically it now scraped the underside of 'barely adequate'. Instead of hidden headlights, the 1970 model opted for four round lights set within the grille. Words completely fail to explain the ugliness of this new styling treatment, which left the Toronado looking cross-eyed and permanently squinting. The Toronado nameplate was phased out in the early 1990s. In 2004 the entire Oldsmobile brand, which dated back to 1897 and had been part of GM since 1908, was dragged out the back and garrotted.

74 Edith

Cheap Trike

As if to prove that not only good things come in small packages, the Australian engineering firm Gray & Harper designed this three-wheeler around 1952.

The company, based in Huntingdale, Victoria, compounded its misdeed three years later by commencing series production. There were mitigating circumstances, however. Gray & Harper didn't produce many and they spared most buyers the bother of even considering the Edith by making it look completely ridiculous.

The Edith was claimed as the first microcar to go into local production and it set new standards for austerity, cartoon styling and misproportioned wheel size. The plan was to sell it for half the price of the country's best-selling family car, the Holden.

Three brave people could be seated on the Edith's bench seat. A rear-mounted 197-cc Villiers two-stroke engine drove the single rear wheel by chain, cleverly eliminating such frivolities as a drive-shaft, a differential and, of course, refinement.

The makers claimed the production version weighed 5 hundredweight and achieved 50 miles per gallon which, when converted into metric (250 kg and 21.25 km/litre), equates to 'terrifyingly light' and 'pretty unimpressive', particularly when you consider a full-sized, four-wheeled, six-cylinder car such as the Holden could better 30 mpg (12.75 km/litre).

Sydney microcar aficionado Fred Diwell is one of the few to experience an Edith first-hand. His verdict is succinct: 'The very worst car I've had the privilege to ride in.'

Australia's first midget was embraced by no person of any size. The seventy-per-year production estimate appears to have peaked at about three or four. If that.

75 Davis

The Boot Scooter

It looked like a full-sized dodgem car. Or perhaps a shoe. It had three wheels, and although claimed as a four-seater, all the passenger seats were arranged in a straight line across one padded bench.

It was to be built by an entirely new company in California (not exactly the heart of the US motor industry) and powered by a Hercules engine normally used for stationary applications, such as roving military spotlights. Stability was questionable, and a weird quirk of the suspension system meant the nose actually rose during heavy braking.

But there was madness in the methods. And fraud, too. Behind the much-hyped 'world's biggest three-wheeler' was one Gary Davis, born in Indiana in 1904 and absolutely, completely and utterly no relation to the author (the author hopes). During the 1920s and 1930s Davis worked as a used-car salesman while assembling an impressive collection of ex-wives, creditors, and disgruntled business partners. Shortly after the Second World War, Davis announced plans to build his own car. One of Davis's claims was that the legendary screen actress Greta Garbo was among his financiers. If a lie, it was an ingenious one, as silent partners couldn't have come much more silent than Garbo. As for the car itself, the origins appear to lie with Frank Kurtis, a racing engineer, who built a three-wheel roadster with a

V8 engine circa 1940. This represented a complete departure from the usual idea that a three-wheeled layout was the domain of underpowered economy cars.

After a scam that enabled Davis to acquire Kurtis's three-wheeler for $50, the vehicle was modified and renamed. Davis's head engineer, Peter Westburg, later described his boss as a 'quick talker

with a ready grin that made you feel at ease. He could borrow the shirt off your back and sell it back to you and you would swear that you had gotten a bargain.'

The unveiling, in 1947, of the oddly curved aluminium-bodied Davis car – to sell for a bargain-basement $995 – came with huge razzle-dazzle. In a series of road shows across the United States in 1947 and 1948 the public was transfixed by such innovations (or gimmicks) as hidden headlights and built-in hydraulic jacks that could raise the body automatically when a tyre needed changing. Indeed, in some places the Davis created almost as much excitement as the bigger, flashier Tucker of the same era.

When people questioned the stability of such a large three-wheeler, Davis paid a Hollywood stunt driver to attempt to turn the car over, apparently without success. Celebrities such as the actor Red Skelton were drafted into the promotional effort, and commission agents, it seems, were taking orders with deposits almost as soon as the prototype was displayed. Hundreds of people also signed on as dealers, which raised as much as $1.2 million.

The Davis was a grab bag of borrowed parts. Many things changed from one car to the next; one early prototype seems to have had a V8 (like the car it was based on), another a six-cylinder, but most were powered by the front-mounted four-cylinder Hercules, which drove the rear wheels. No matter which engine was fitted, however, Davis's claim of '100 mph and 50 mpg' (160 km/h and 21.25 km/litre) was nonsense of the utter variety.

Many people believe that Preston Tucker, for all his shortcomings, intended to build and sell his controversial Tucker 48. Fewer believe Davis had any such plans for his car. There was plenty of money coming in but little evidence that it was being spent on the things needed to meet the proposed production schedule of 50 cars per day in 1947, ramping up to 100 a day in 1948. The things Davis did spend company money on, according to court records, included a Beverly Hills home for himself, mink coats for acquaintances (presumably female), and various other items not entirely necessary for volume automotive production. And by one account none of Davis's workers ever received paycheques for their efforts.

By 1948, those who had purchased dealer franchises were screaming for cars that never seemed to arrive, and legal authorities were trying to unravel the highly creative corporate structure that had been devised. They succeeded, and in 1949, the man with his name on the bodywork was hauled off to jail for fraud and the car-making operation wound up. Just seventeen Davis cars had been built; Davis himself was released after two years and died in 1973.

76 VW Country Buggy

Sink, Sank, Sunk

There are many curious things about the VW Country Buggy. But nothing is curiouser than the fact it was designed to rescue a company that couldn't make money building the world's most successful car.

The story goes something like this: when the VW Beetle became an unexpected hit in Australia during the 1950s, local assembly commenced and plans were laid for a full-scale manufacturing operation in Clayton, Victoria.

Volkswagen Australasia Pty Ltd (VWA) was formed in 1957, the first sheet-metal panels were produced in 1960, and by 1967 most Beetle mechanical components were also Australian-made. The only problem was that, as VWA's investment increased in pursuit of 95 per cent local content, Beetle sales fell in almost perfect unison. The bottom line required 50,000 cars a year. At no time did VWA come even close to achieving it.

As the local operation drowned in red ink, the Aussie Beetle was deprived of even the modest styling and mechanical updates fitted to German versions. More modern offerings, including the Mini Minor and a new breed of Japanese cars, grabbed an increasing share of the budget car market.

So what was the answer? VWA's director of quality control Rudi Herzmer thought it was a unique-to-Australia, 'go anywhere' vehicle loosely modelled on the German Army Kubelwagen, which he had worked on. The fruit of Herzmer's idea used standard Beetle mechanical components and was announced in February 1967. What's more, like the delightfully named Schwimmwagen variant of the Second World War military vehicle, the Australian vehicle would be amphibious.

The project was conceived in such a rush that VWA released photos of the vehicle before it had even finalised a name. A press preview of the incredible floating VW – temporarily dubbed 'The Thing' – was held at Hume Weir, near Albury, New South Wales. While Herzmer seriously lobbied for the Kubelwagen name, some journalists suggested instead that it was a blend of Jeep and Moke and should be called Joke.

When the production version was released several months later, it had acquired the uninspiring handle of 'Country Buggy'. The base price had been set at Aus$1,550. The engine choice was between the 1.2-litre and 1.3-litre Dak-Dak units, while buyers could specify a four-speed manual gearbox . . . or a four-speed manual gearbox. Other options included buying the Country Buggy, and not buying it.

In this spirit, a printed summary issued to the press remarked that 'little consideration has been given to expensive and useless adornment'. Test-drivers of this crude and hard-to-love vehicle were to soon find that little consideration had been given to many other aspects as well. The Country Buggy's motive power went strictly to the rear; the fact that the engine was directly over the drive wheels was supposedly enough to justify the 'go anywhere' tag. One place the production version of the new VeeDub wouldn't go, however, was across a pond. The amphibious capability had been quietly dropped following directives from the German factory. The crucial word here is quietly, because at least one unknowing motor magazine test crew drove a Country Buggy down a boat ramp and sank.

Another place the Country Buggy refused to go was out of a showroom door. Despite the addition of the incredible (non-floating) Country Buggy, VWA managed to sell just 11,000 vehicles of all varieties in 1968, and that total included only 842 Country Buggys. The game was up. VWA dropped the Buggy and the Aussie-made Beetle, wrote off Aus$20 million in plant and equipment and returned the Clayton plant to a simple assembly operation. The factory was eventually sold to Nissan, which managed to lose so much money building cars there (up to Aus$1 billion), that VW's problems seemed almost minor in comparison.

77 Prenvic

Steerage

We know this car was built in Belgrade in 1959, but we're not entirely sure why. The best guess is that the Prenvic's curious diamond-pattern wheel arrangement was executed to win a bet. That, or to harness the advantages that have been claimed for the layout on the two or three other times people have been silly enough to adopt it. These include: a smaller turning circle (feasible), better aerodynamics (vaguely possible), more useable space (doubtful) and greater stability (you've got to be joking).

The styling was curious: a bit of Chrysler Airlow at the front, a tiny hint of filed-down Cadillac at the rear and a four-slice Toast-o-Matic in between. Sketchy mechanical details suggest the Prenvic's single front wheel turned in unison with its single rear wheel. The other two wheels, meanwhile, were cleverly positioned to be completely in the way of the doors.

78 Jensen Interceptor

Going for Broke

By the time the Jensen Interceptor appeared in 1966, the practice of cramming large American engines into English sports cars was already firmly established. And when it came to finding a large piece of US iron, Jensen – an English coach-building firm with a heritage going back to the 1920s – didn't muck about. It started with a 6.2-litre Chrysler V8 and soon moved up to a 7.2-litre version.

The 1966 Interceptor was based on the previous Jensen C-V8 model (from 1962), with a body worked on by Italy's Touring studio and Vignale. Visually, the most spectacular thing was the hatchback tail with its huge rear fishbowl window.

On the road it proved large, heavy, luxurious and quick. The fastest version could touch 140 mph (225 km/h). But promoting it from interesting to remarkable was the fact that a four-wheel drive version (known as the 'FF') was also produced.

Using an innovative centre differential system developed by tractor magnate Harry Ferguson, the Interceptor FF was the world's first four-wheel-drive, high-performance car, and led to a whole new philosophy about how to get the most high-speed traction and performance. Or to put it in more cynical terms, on-road four-wheel drive enabled owners to lose control at an even greater speed, in the same way that a good off-road four-wheel-drive system allows people to become bogged down in even more inaccessible places.

Four-wheel drive wasn't all that set the FF apart. Distinguished from the standard model by a slightly longer wheelbase and an extra vent or gill behind each front wheel, the Interceptor FF matched its four-wheel drive with Dunlop Maxaret anti-skid brakes, originally developed for jet planes. These two major innovations were described by Jensen as 'mechanical guardian angels'.

The two-wheel drive and FF models both had as standard a three-speed auto box (also from Chrysler) though a four-speed could be specified. There were four seats, although the two rear seats were not suitable for people with legs.

Despite its guardian angels, the FF version couldn't be saved. It was as dear as it was complicated (in both cases, far too) and production ceased with just 318 examples built. The rear-drive version continued, but by the early 1970s a two-wheel-drive Jensen Interceptor Series III cost markedly more than a Porsche 911 or V12 Jaguar E-Type.

Like so many British cars, the Jensen suffered a litany of electrical woes, suspension problems and engine overheating (with resulting melting of under-bonnet hoses and wires). Rust was never very far away. The engine capacity guaranteed profligate fuel use, and the early 1970s brought both a fuel shock and a collapse of the British economy. Neither helped sales of a 7.2-litre car.

The Interceptor convertible and coupé models (the latter a seemingly pointless 'fixed head' version of the former) were launched in 1974 and 1975 respectively, by which time Jensen was in

receivership. It was a victim of a changing market, British industrial relations, the oil crisis, the cost of the Interceptor development and the disastrous Jensen-Healey project. In 1976 Jensen experienced the first of several closedowns, but in 1983 the company climbed back up on to its elbows and, amazingly, managed to crawl forward until the early 1990s before succumbing to the inevitable.

The final Series IV Interceptor was priced in the UK at £100,000, compared with the original price of £3,742. At neither price, though, was it profitable.

79 Panther 6

More Is Less

It was in England in 1972 that Panther Westwinds Ltd commenced business, if selling cars at a financial loss can be called a business. As well as blending a Rolls-Royce and Triumph Dolomite in its strange and unnecessary Rio model, Panther made an even odder contribution to the motoring world of the 1970s.

It was a 1977 sports machine known as the 6, on account of its having 50 per cent more wheels than most people expected when they bought a car. The idea of a six-wheel road car wasn't entirely new. A few cross-country vehicles had been built with an extra axle, just in case. But the Panther was certainly the first sports car thus equipped; its three pairs of wheels were said to be there for improved on-road acceleration, braking, and handling.

The downside of the unusual layout was that it cost more and nobody really needed it. But that seemed a small consideration when you saw how much press was generated by the announcement of this vehicle.

The idea was already proven, up to a point, by the Tyrrell racing team, which had won a Grand Prix the previous year with a six-wheel Formula One car. Tyrrell used conventional wheels at the rear, but tiny wheels on the front, reducing the height – and therefore the aerodynamic drag – of the front end. It also put more rubber on the road for greater cornering grip. The Panther 6, however, used almost the same-size wheels on the front as the back and was thus burdened with many of the disadvantages of having six wheels – extra weight, complexity and rolling resistance – without a profile that afforded a really low ground-hugging nose. And, to house a 7.9-litre Cadillac V8 with twin turbochargers, the Panther 6 had the longest tail in the automotive kingdom.

The overall styling treatment brought to mind Lady Penelope's car in the original *Thunderbirds* television series. Between the long nose and even longer tail was a tiny two-seater cockpit nestled behind a vast windshield. The instruments were digital and there was a television and phone, plenty of leather and suede, and very little elbow room.

The quoted price was a then-monstrous £40,000, but it was said that fifteen orders were taken at the British Motor Fair of 1977.

A year later the company's owner, former fashion designer Robert Jankel (pictured here with the 6), seemed no closer to fulfilling orders, so he arranged for some car magazines to have supervised access to the car, presumably in the hope that this would convince the doubters. Jankel first explained to the road testers that the production delays were due to Pirelli not supplying the right tyres, so some special allowances had to be made for the handling idiosyncrasies. Proper suspension calibration could only be done with the final tyres, he said.

Under the heading 'Is it a bird? Is it a plane? Is it a joke?' *The Motor* took to the wheel and – having identified various unusual handling tendencies on a straight stretch of road – threw the Panther 6 into a corner. 'Certainly the sheer adhesion of all that rubber is tremendous,' the venerable British magazine concluded, 'but at high cornering speeds you are very much aware of the huge mass of engine behind you, threatening to swing the tail out like a massive pendulum.'

The magazine's test driver also found the steering uncommunicative, the brakes lacking, and the acceleration from rest less than expected of such an enormous engine; he also detected a tendency for the front tyres to 'tramline', or follow grooves in the road. Yet the journalist still walked away seemingly of the opinion that some new tyres and a tune-up of the carburettor would calm the savage beast. 'There is some fine honing to be done [but] it works, it's for real, and it's beautifully made,' was the remarkably soft conclusion.

Panther never had the chance to prove the case. Series production never eventuated, supposedly because of the problem with obtaining tyres. Rather than buyers. By 1980 the company was in receivership.

80 AMC Gremlin

Coupe de Vile

Described by its maker as 'the first US designed and built small car which will compete directly with leading imports', this bout of dismay on wheels was essentially the front half of a Rambler Hornet combined with a weird-as-all-get-out chopped tail. This gave the Gremlin all the disadvantages of its larger AMC stablemate, but less interior room.

Designer Richard Teague reputedly sketched the lines of this 1970 offering on the back of an airline sickbag. And as a final brave touch, AMC decided to christen it with a synonym for trouble. *Webster's Unabridged Dictionary* (Random House edition), for example, defines a gremlin as 'a mischievous invisible being, said by airplane pilots in World War II to cause engine trouble and mechanical difficulties'.

And having decided to build a smaller car – and, in tautological fashion, call it a subcompact – how did AMC power it? With the same engines as bigger models. The base donk was a 3.3-litre (199-cubic-inch) six-cylinder, while a V8 was optional.

The cheapest version, known as the Commuter, had seats only in the front and sold poorly. The four-seater did slightly better, despite the rear seats being tiny and the occupants often feeling imprisoned behind those huge rear pillars. From a driver's point of view, these pillars created perhaps the biggest blind spot of any American car, while the Gremlin's nose-heavy nature made the handling abominable, particularly with the V8.

The Gremlin was dead in the water by 1978, despite such innovations as 'hockey stick' side stripes, and a Levi's Custom Trim option with seats upholstered in nylon meant to look like denim, and punctuated by rivets meant to look like copper. Just before its demise, AMC finally decided to offer a four-cylinder Gremlin. But it was too late and, considering the model's porky weight, it was also too little.

81 Volvo 760 GLE

Thinking Inside the Square

Sweden's Volvo company went into the 1980s with a car from the 1960s. However, with the 1982 launch of the first totally new Volvo in more than fifteen years, the company was promising a revolutionary car for the 1990s and beyond. That car, the 760 GLE, was intended as the bold and striking model that would distinguish Volvo from every other make and enable the brand to soar upmarket and take on BMW and Mercedes-Benz.

The truth, though, was that the 760 GLE was a pug-ugly tank of a saloon that did the company damage from which it has, arguably, yet to recover.

The new-for-the-1980s Volvo was perhaps the boxiest mass-produced car ever launched. There was scarcely a curved line to be found anywhere on it, and those cumbersome chrome mouldings along its bodywork seemed to speak of an earlier, unloved era. Even on the inside, the square and bulky instrument panel of old had been redesigned – to make it even squarer and bulkier.

'It will look good,' quipped Rover's head stylist, Roy Axe, 'once they take it out of the packing crate.'

Volvo officials offered rejoinders such as, 'Not everyone wants to drive a jellybean on wheels', but it seemed that more people wanted to do that than drive a Volvo 760. The irony was that in order to see

what an outsider could do, Volvo had originally commissioned
Italdesign to style the body. The directors looked at the rounded,
thoroughly modern Italian proposition and rejected it in favour of the
work of its own designers. D'oh!

At the time it launched the 760, the Swedish firm was bullish,
having just finished its most successful year ever, a year in which it
had sold over 300,000 saloons and station wagons. The plan to move
further upmarket was less to do with hubris than with the fact that the
bottom end of the luxury market was being swamped with Japanese

cars that were well made, generously equipped, and a lot cheaper than anything coming out of Sweden.

The 760 GLE had a longer wheelbase and a wider track than the 200 series it partially replaced. Technically, it was business as usual: front engine, rear drive. The slightly revolutionary auto trannie with push-button overdrive came from Japan. The standard engine was the 2.8-litre V6, as used in the older 264 model. There was a high luxury specification and, in the Volvo tradition, lots of practical features and safety equipment.

Volvo had claimed that 'the science of aerodynamics has played a major part in shaping the car's strikingly different body design'.

But the drag coefficient figure turned out to be 0.39, which equates roughly to that of a barn. Travelling sideways. Indeed, the drag coefficient was so decidedly unflash that when a wagon version was later produced, it cut through the air more efficiently than the saloon.

That sales of the 760 started with a bang merely reflected the long wait since the last all-new Volvo. They stopped soon afterwards with a veritable nuclear explosion.

In response to barbs in the press about the styling, Volvo issued a statement saying: '[We] do not follow trends because they often turn out to be just trends . . . The 760 GLE will absolutely not look as dated in a few years as some cars with rounded teardrop shapes introduced lately.'

Despite this assertion, what followed over the next few years was a desperate attempt by Volvo to round off all the 760 edges and make the car look more like the 'rounded teardrop shapes introduced lately'. But the company always seemed one step behind.

82 Alfa Romeo 33

Alfasud's Last Sprout

The Alfa 33, first seen in 1983, was the replacement for the horror and wonder that was the Alfasud. On the days it was working, the Sud was possessed of a certain charm and delightful road manners. But it established a new benchmark for 'shortgevity'. Rust was the main problem, but there were scores of others, many of which were carried across to the thirsty, unreliable, badly built 33.

The 33 was, after all, a Sud with a new five-door hatchback body from Pininfarina, rather than a much-needed all-new design. The Sud antecedents gave the 33 a glorious 'flat four' engine, nimble road manners and very little else to commend it.

The various 33s driven by this author exhibited the sort of unfathomable faults that only Alfa could produce. One had an interior light that came on during heavy braking. And for a small car, the 33 was surprisingly noisy. Some of the hullabaloo was a sporty engine note, but more of it was the squeaking, shaking and groaning of badly fitted components. No wonder some thought the model designation was a mark out of a hundred.

Like many other Alfas, the 33 offered a driving position aimed at creatures further down the evolutionary chain. Drivers with arms less than twice the length of their legs were especially uncomfortable. But at least the driver's footwell was roomy. This was because the three

pedals were grouped as tightly as piano keys in the left corner. The steering wheel too was offset.

The car was restyled in 1987 and then again in 1990, by which stage the platform was going on twenty years old and the car around it was feeling like a bad meal relived ('still a severely flawed package' concluded *Autocar & Motor*). The restyle for the 1990s gave the model a lower nose and a higher tail. Just in case you still had any rearward vision, many models had an aero-wing blocking the bottom of the rear screen and a high-mounted brake light concealing the top.

By this stage, variations of the 33 had acquired such outlandish monikers as the Alfa 33 Boxer 16 Valve QV hatchback, while the one-time Giardinetta wagon had been renamed SportWagon, probably to take attention away from the fact that it had very little carrying capacity. The four-cylinder 'boxer' engine had been drawn out to 1.7 litres to produce a very peaky 98 kW (131 bhp), plus even more noise and torque steer. A four-wheel-drive version was also available. This had the added appellation of 33S P4, and more buttons to play with while you waited for roadside assistance.

Alfa Romeo sales were by this time in dire straits, yet the 33 had four more years to run before a Fiat Tipo-based replacement was ready. The chaos was hardly a surprise. A few years earlier an Alfa Romeo chief planner had dismissed the entire Asian motor industry with the line: 'The Japanese could never build an Alfa Romeo.' If the 33 was anything to go by, neither could the Italians.

83 Scamp

Charged and Found Guilty

During the 1960s and early 1970s it was generally agreed that if you were going to build an electric car, it had to be tiny, demonstrably unstable, and/or unspeakably ugly. Better still, all three.

Which brings us to the Scamp. This two-seater fibreglass-bodied micro is described in some circles as 'the last car solely conceived, designed, and built in Scotland'.

Don't be fooled by the Cyclops eye and trinket styling, these people were serious. They thought they could take on the Mini Minor, the Hillman Minx, and other British small cars with an electric vehicle possessing just two seats, a miserable range of about 32 kilometres (20 miles) between charges, and a price that was dangerously close to that of a real car.

The Scamp was designed to keep Scottish Aviation engineers busy after production of the twin-engined Prestwick Pioneer aeroplane came to an end, circa 1964. Finance was provided by the Electricity Council, which intended to sell the Scamp next to washing machines and light fittings in its high street showrooms.

Stirling Moss, who was no stranger to spruiking British cars that had plenty of room for improvement, loaned or rented some kind words, but it wasn't enough. The Scamp was absolutely flat biscuit at about 60 km/h (35 mph) on the level, with one occupant. The old-fashioned lead-acid batteries – wired up to a salvaged aeroplane starter motor – were expensive to replace and needed recharging far too frequently.

Worse still, the Electricity Council insisted on independent safety evaluation by the Motor Industry Research Association. When the Scamp's suspension collapsed during the tests that followed, it made many people glad they weren't 16,000 feet up in something else made by Scottish Aviation. The rather spectacular failure also led to the Electricity Council unplugging itself from the project.

Scottish Aviation continued for a while, but only eleven or twelve Scamps were made.

84 Tucker 48

Damned Torpedo

The Tucker 48 appears in some lists of the Greatest Cars Ever Built, and the man behind this late 1940s streamliner – a Michigan-born former car salesman named Preston Thomas Tucker – is the subject of the idolatrous film *Tucker: The Man and his Dream*, directed by no less a figure than Francis Ford Coppola.

The true believers will tell you that Mr T was visionary, his car revolutionary and the whole venture a noble attempt to break Detroit's thoroughly evil car-making cartel. This retelling suggests that the Tucker car was festooned with technological and safety features that major makers had conspired to suppress, and the government joined in on the plot to bring the upstart company down. In this David and Goliath battle, Goliath was not only bigger, he was the one with the slingshot.

The case for the prosecution paints Tucker as a shady character who wasted most of the millions he raised from mum-and-dad investors while pursuing a fanciful and even fraudulent project.

The story started in 1946, when Tucker unveiled a sketch of his 'Torpedo', and claimed this was a 'car of the future for the everyday man', one that had already been the subject of fifteen years of development. It was a good time to sell a dream; with the war over and a scarcity of new cars, there was pent-up demand and plenty of

blue-sky optimism. Investors and potential dealers threw their money –
a remarkable US$26 million of it – at the tall and charming man in a
sharp suit. Even the War Assets Administration did a highly favourable
deal on a massive factory in Chicago.

The Torpedo prototype, now called the Tucker 48, was unveiled
amid great showmanship in July 1947. However, beneath the glitz and
gloss it was a hurriedly thrown together effort to placate increasingly
nervous investors and the Securities and Exchange Commission
(SEC), which had begun taking a keen interest in Tucker's business
manoeuvres.

Under Tucker's guidance, the designer Alex Tremulis drew up the
body and produced something that looked slightly ahead of Detroit's
mainstream efforts. However, it was hardly the leap into the distant
future promised by the early sketches. One notable feature was a
centre headlight that turned with the wheels, but the prototype lacked
the disc brakes and seatbelts Tucker had boasted about. Of the safety

features that were present, the so-called crash padding on the dash was of dubious value, and the provision of an area into which the front-seat passenger could duck before a collision was just plain silly.

And despite Tucker's claims that the 48 was 'the first completely new car in 50 years', the prototype's transmission had been salvaged from a pre-war Cord and its body fabricated around a 1942 Oldsmobile. The SEC would soon argue that the Tucker operation had neither the expertise nor the serious intention to turn this hand-built one-off into a series production car.

As for the mechanical layout, what worked for the Volkswagen Beetle became the stuff of low comedy when what you hung over the back axle was a huge 'six' with a capacity of 589 cubic inches, or 9.65 litres. This massively heavy but not overly powerful engine needed two truck batteries to turn it over. If such a tail-heavy machine wasn't going to go around corners very happily – even with the smaller 5.5-litre

(335-cubic-inch) donk that replaced the original 589 – the Tucker should at least have been good in a straight line. The later engine was designed for a helicopter and supposedly produced 123 kW (165 bhp), compared with the Chevy six's 67 kW (90 bhp). On the other hand, the Tucker weighed more than 2 tonnes and Tucker's claimed '130 mph (209 km/h) top speed' and '35 miles per gallon' (12.4 km/litre) fuel economy were highly suspect.

A pilot production run of fifty cars was pushed through to convince investors and the SEC, which stepped up its investigations when Mr T raised yet more money with an advance purchase plan on accessories. The fifty cars were hand-built at monumental expense, yet the price was a bargain $2,450.

In 1948 Tucker published an open letter outlining his woes. His factory, he wrote, was infiltrated with industrial spies while his efforts were being undermined by competitors with friends 'in high places in Washington'. He suggested elsewhere that other car makers were bullying their suppliers into withholding parts. In reality, Tucker was years away from being in a position to order parts in serious quantities.

Tucker and his associates went to trial on thirty-one charges of fraud but were eventually found not guilty. It was little consolation, because by then the Tucker concern was thoroughly bankrupt. In 1951 the man at the centre of it all did what any man in his circumstances would. He flew to Brazil to seek financial backing for another new car. This time it was a sports model called Carioca, but it still hadn't come to fruition when Tucker died of cancer in 1956, aged fifty-three.

85 Ford Pinto

Passengers Alight Here

The Pinto 'subcompact' was named after a horse. A piebald horse. A piebald horse with a tendency, one assumes, to explode.

The Ford that would become known as 'the barbecue that seats four' was rushed to market for the 1971 model year as a counter to Chevrolet's equally unexciting but considerable less flammable Vega.

There was nothing innovative about the Pinto's styling or engineering, but the price was right, the four-cylinder engine was reasonably economical, and sales were strong. But by 1974 Ralph Nader's Center for Auto Safety was demanding a recall, arguing that the Pinto's tendency to concertina in rear-end accidents did more than rip open the badly positioned fuel tank. It tended to jam the doors shut.

At first only a two-door Pinto saloon was offered, but the range was soon expanded to include a Runabout model. This featured a hatch door at the rear, presumably to give easier access to the rescue crews.

Despite rising concerns about Pinto safety, Ford refused to change a thing, offering the Department of Transportation such inventive arguments as 'retooling for the changes would take 43 months' (considerably longer than it had taken to develop the entire car) and – wait for it – 'most of those people were already dead from the impact before the fire started'.

Ford's reluctance to modify was perhaps driven by arrogance, but also by the high cost of new tooling and the fact that a different fuel tank would compromise boot space (an important selling feature). Yet the Pinto continued to ignite debate – and motorists – and Ford even launched a 'woody wagon' version. Sure, its sides were covered with plastic woodgrain rather than real timber, but it still seemed to be adding fuel to the fire.

In 1977, however, the growing band of Pintonista rebels received their manifesto. It was a brilliant piece of investigative journalism by Mark Dowie in *Mother Jones* magazine, the journal of the Foundation for National Progress (Mother Jones was a celebrated nineteenth-century labour leader).

Using internal Ford documents and hundreds of collision reports, this article (now archived on motherjones.com) detailed how Ford had conducted its own crash tests and was aware of the hazards awaiting those early buyers. Yet, Dowie wrote, Ford refused to modify the Pinto and even rejected as too expensive a one-dollar plastic shield that significantly reduced chances of the exposed fuel tank being punctured. Ford had a design brief that demanded the car weigh 'not an ounce over 2,000 pounds nor cost a cent over $2,000' and was grimly sticking to it.

Dowie wrote that, despite as many as 900 deaths in Pinto fires, Henry Ford II continued to campaign vigorously against new safety legislation. 'Compliance to these standards will shut down the industry,' Henry II said repeatedly. But what made the most impact with the public was *Mother Jones*'s detailing of Ford's now-notorious 'cost-benefit analysis'. This assigned a value to each fatality of $200,000 and to each serious burning of $67,000 and argued that the cost of changing the Pinto exceeded the cost of deaths and maimings (when calculated in such a way).

Ford said the *Mother Jones* article was filled with 'distortions and half-truths', but nevertheless recalled 1.5 million Pintos. Shortly after this recall started, cost-benefit analysis calculations were blown to bits when a Californian jury awarded a Pinto victim, Richard Grimshaw, a record US$125 million in punitive damages. A year later Indiana prosecutors charged Ford Motor Company executives with reckless homicide.

The Pinto's own funeral pyre was lit in 1980. The Grimshaw judgement was later reduced on appeal (to $3.5 million), the executives were acquitted on the reckless homicide charges, and, strangely, none of the fuss ever greatly hurt Pinto sales. So perhaps Ford was right all along: a low purchase price and a boot that takes a second set of golf clubs *is* better than a long life and happy retirement.

86 Mazda Roadpacer AP

The Bloatary

It seems almost inconceivable today that a Japanese car maker planning a new range-topping luxury car would turn to the Australian arm of General Motors for the body. But Mazda did exactly that in 1975, putting its logo loudly and proudly on a rebadged Holden Premier.

The Roadpacer was announced on 1 April – a date that may or may not have any special symbolism in the Land of the Rising Sun – and although the exterior was familiar, the car had been completely re-engineered to take a Mazda 13B Wankel rotary engine.

The Roadpacer was intended only for the Japanese market and every gadget and gizmo in Mazda's armoury was brought to battle. The Roadpacer had central locking, power steering, dual-zone air conditioning and a car refrigerator. Although top speed was claimed to be 95 mph (152 km/h), at 55 mph (88.5 km/h) a loud musical tone sounded. This was presumably to remind Japanese drivers that they had an additional 40 mph (64 km/h) up their sleeve. Other Mazda changes included softening the suspension to the point that the chassis bottomed out regularly on anything approaching a rough road.

Why a heavy and space-inefficient Holden body was chosen for a lightweight and compact engine is hard to say. The net result was a car that was far more expensive to produce, yet no quicker than the pushrod six-cylinder Holden it was based on. Furthermore, Japan was still suffering severely from the energy shock, and the Wankel engine drank like a salaryman at the end of a long week. The Roadpacer was also too broad for many Japanese streets, and it was hit with the special 'wide-car tax'. This was one of those curious and mysteriously changing levies the Japanese government used to ensure that the country's 'open market' would remain almost completely free of imports.

The Wankel was the engine that helped send Mazda bankrupt and the unloved Roadpacer was killed off a few months before Ford bailed out the company by purchasing 25 per cent of its shares. If not for the success of the 1979 RX-7, Mazda's rotary-engine programme would almost certainly have died as well.

87 Nash Metropolitan

Cold Comfort

No other vehicle in history has managed as convincing an impersonation of a prostrate refrigerator on castor wheels as the Nash Metropolitan. Perhaps then, it's no surprise that this car came from the corporation that also built Kelvinator kitchen appliances.

The Metropolitan's Toyland appearance would later make it a collectable, but the car completely failed to be popular in its day. This was despite intensive market research that appeared to show that such a vehicle was just what American motorists of the 1950s were waiting for.

In many people's minds it was all Austin's fault. This is grossly unfair. Yes, the Austin Motor Company did build the Metropolitan, and it did so at its Longbridge plant in England. But it built the car entirely under contract, and to a US template. The styling was the work of an independent designer, William Flajole, who – I'm guessing here – hoped people would take the Metropolitan home because they felt sorry for it.

It was a lack of expertise in the small-car field, and of the right production facilities, that led to the Nash-Kelvinator group outsourcing the manufacturing to the company considered the international leader in small cars at that time. And so, from early 1954, this most un-American of American vehicles arrived on US shores direct from

Austin. A two-door hardtop and a convertible were offered. Both were short, narrow, and top-heavy, with only a hint of wheel arches. There was also a strange notch in each door, which, taking into account the refrigerator heritage, might have been modelled on a dairy compartment.

The Metropolitan was generously equipped, but not particularly cheap, despite its modest size and the fact the Pound Sterling was then held in the same esteem as British dentistry. The body was of a

monocoque, or unitary, construction type. The spare tyre was on the tail, then considered a European touch. There was a contrasting roof colour, and eventually an elaborate two-tone paint job.

Under the bonnet was Austin's tiny (by American standards) 1.2-litre four-cylinder A40 engine. The 0-to-60 mph sprint was more like a stroll. It took around 30 seconds. To market such a small, low-powered, curiously styled vehicle in the States in the 1950s was brave. An increasing number of American cars had twice as many cylinders and four times the engine capacity.

A second wind – okay, gentle breeze – was provided in 1956 by a 1.5-litre Metropolitan with revised styling, improved equipment levels, and 25 per cent more power. But sales numbers continued to be modest (to put it politely), and perhaps reached even that level only because it was almost impossible to slake America's thirst for new cars in the 1950s.

Within a couple of months of the first Metropolitan going on sale, Nash had merged with Hudson to form American Motors Corporation, so some Hudson-brand Metropolitans were also sold before 1957, after which the new concern decided to concentrate on the Rambler brand. At this point the Nash and Hudson nameplates were dropped and the car became simply 'the Metropolitan'. It was also marketed under that simple moniker in the UK when Austin purchased the right to sell it in the home market. Or, more correctly, the right to fail to sell it in the home market.

The Metropolitan was finally hit on the head with a brick in 1961, though unsold stock kept showrooms full until well into 1962.

88 Daimler SP250

Strange Fish

With a heritage dating to the 1890s, the Daimler company had worked hard to shape its reputation as a maker of staid, solid, luxurious conveyances. And it maintained that reputation right up until 1959 when the venerable British company's corporate brain fell out and it decided to release the SP250.

The first and only sports car to wear a Daimler logo wasn't just any old roadster. It was the oddest-looking one in the sports-car world, with bug eyes sticking out of a strangely curved nose and a radiator grille that looked like the mouth of some obscure species of bottom-feeding marine life.

The slab sides were broken up by oddly protruding wheel arches and there was a step in the profile to make way for fins that didn't so much as blend in as blend out. But there was one thing uglier than an SP250 with the top down: an SP250 with its tall, square, ill-fitting canvas roof in the 'up' position.

Aimed squarely at the US market, which was then grabbing every British sports car it could get its hands on, Daimler's roadster was launched as the Dart at the 1959 New York Motor Show. Chrysler had registered the name Dart and demanded that the Daimler name be withdrawn. It could have performed a bigger service for humanity by demanding that the whole car be withdrawn.

'Breathtaking as its performance is Dart's styling!' boasted the original, clumsily worded brochure. 'From sleek, fluted grill to flaunting rear fins, every eye-appealing curve of its polyester body expresses the spirit of speed.'

The copy would have served better to deceive if it hadn't been placed directly under an illustration of those allegedly eye-appealing curves. Still, the newcomer had disc brakes, which was unusual, and a home-grown V8 engine, which for a British car was even more so. This 2.54-litre overhead-camshaft unit was developed from a 'V Twin' Triumph motorcycle engine. Despite this – and the fact it was originally meant to be air-cooled (leading to an under-the-bonnet spaghetti of cooling hoses on early versions) – the V8 worked surprisingly well and spat out a healthy 105 kW (140 bhp). The problem was the car around it.

The SP250 exhibited atrocious wobbling and shuddering because of a lack of body rigidity. *Autocar* magazine noted that the driver's door tended to pop open during hard cornering. The omission of bumpers as standard equipment was curious, while handling was average at best and extremely dependent on the right tyre pressures. Top speed, though, was 193 km/h, or a shade under 120 mph. That impressive figure was helped along by the lightness of the polyester body. Which, presumably, never needed ironing.

By the way, the English company was called Daimler because in 1893 Frederick Simms negotiated to build German Daimler vehicles under licence in Britain. In 1926, the original German company, Daimler Motoren-Gesellschaft (formed by Gottlieb Daimler in Cannstatt, near Stuttgart, in 1890) merged with the company started by Karl Benz to become Daimler-Benz. Benz's company had already established the name Mercedes, so the Mercedes-Benz name was used for cars from the merged company. The British firm, dubbed the Daimler Motor Company in 1896, stuck with the Daimler name.

For Britain's Daimler, the SP250 ended up not so much an exciting sports adventure as a death throe. In 1960 the company was swallowed by Jaguar. As Jaguar was in the process of preparing its E-Type model for market it had little need for a fish as strange as the SP250. However, orders had been received from American dealers, so a decision was taken to proceed with production of the Daimler SP250 and hope for the best.

The best did not eventuate. The US market may have been grabbing every British sports car available, but it was prepared to make an exception in this case. After about a year, Jaguar engineers heavily reinforced the SP250's body to stop its scuttle shake. Bumpers became standard equipment. However, the body reinforcement didn't eliminate cracking panels, drooping doors and other problems. What wasn't polyester still had a tendency to rust. And what didn't rust remained unspeakably ugly.

Only 1,200 SP250s were sold in left-hand-drive markets, including to Americans, for whose tastes the styling had supposedly been created. The grand total of all sales, before production officially spluttered to a halt in 1964, was a miserable 2,645 units.

89 Moller Skycar

Flight of Fancy

Ever since humans have been able to drive and fly, inventors have tried to produce a vehicle that will do both. It's been mostly the stuff of meat and pastry in the firmament, though in 1951 the Aerocar achieved limited success. Never mind that its wings had to be carried in a trailer about as long as a small bus, or that nobody bought it. It could fly, after a fashion, and drive, after another.

Canadian-born Dr Paul Moller has spent more than thirty years and close to US$100 million working on his George Jetson-like, eight-engined, vertical-take-off Skycar. He has taken it around the world to talk about (rather than demonstrate) its cloud-hopping, distance-eating capabilities, which he claims include 564 km/h (350 mph) cruising with hatchback economy.

Despite decades of hype – the first order was taken in 1974 – the Skycar has never flown for more than a minute, and then only on the end of a rope. Still, Moller reckons he'll untether his creation and hit 350 mph soon. At present only one Skycar exists, but Moller says once production hits half a million units a year the price will come down to that of a mid-size luxury car. In the meantime the race is on to see which flies first: the Moller or the pig.

90 Austin Freeway

Six Doesn't Sell

It shared its name with a big road in Texas and had fins just like an American car from the 1950s. But the Austin Freeway of the early 1960s was loudly and proudly advertised as being made by and for Australians. Unfortunately there were more Australians in the 'by' than 'for' category.

The British Motor Company, or BMC, launched the Freeway in 1962 in a dismally misguided attempt to take on the local six-cylinder family cars from GM (Holden), Ford (Falcon) and Chrysler (Valiant). This attempt was based on the dodgy notion that the success the company had enjoyed with the Mini Minor could be carried up the scale.

Loosely based on the styling of the Austin Farina A60 (and just as loosely built), the Freeway was available in saloon and wagon versions. But whereas the A60 had tried to command a Holden price with a four-cylinder engine, this was a six – and the Freeway was equipped with features not standard on most other cars of the day, including windscreen washers and a fresh-air heater/demister unit.

An earlier attempt to Australianise a British car, the 1957 Morris Marshall, had featured a thoroughly unconvincing boomerang on the radiator grille. The Freeway didn't win any further points for its tizzy little map of Australia in the centre of its steering wheel.

Like most things to do with the new Austin, the unique, locally built engine was a shortcut, being merely an extended version of the A60's 1.6-litre four. Existing factory machinery was used to machine the longer block, saving money. In a similar spirit of making do, the rear fins were taken from Riley and MG saloons (BMC also used these brand-names on a confusing mix of similar cars with different badges

and more upmarket detailing). The bonnet was from the A60 but with an extra bit welded to the leading edge and the join hidden behind the favourite decorative device of the day: a chrome strip.

The reason the Freeway was an Austin was because the latest incarnation of BMC's ever-changing model strategy was to sell its mainstream small cars under the Morris name, family cars as Austins, and luxury vehicles as Wolseleys. Hence a Wolseley version of the Freeway was also built. To help this along, it was given the emotive and instantly memorable name of 24/80. Yes, 24/80.

The Freeway/Wolseley 2.4-litre engine was described as 'the Blue Streak six', which might have been appropriate if oil was blue. Freeway reliability problems included leaks, shrieks and some fairly spectacular engine seizures.

The sales slogan was 'Make way for the Austin Freeway'. Australians did more than that. They gave it the widest berth possible. Precisely 3,090 Freeways were sold in the first year, which was also the most successful year. Or least unsuccessful year. To appreciate the size of the failure, consider that the car BMC perceived as the direct competitor, the Holden, sold more examples each and every week than the Freeway had managed in an entire year.

Even fewer Freeways were pushed through the door in year two. In October 1964, a Mark II version was launched, but nobody cared. The name Wolseley disappeared from the market soon afterwards, and Freeway production was discontinued in 1965. Despite this, the company would come back three more times with a local six-cylinder car in the vainglorious hope of taking on the well-entrenched American makes Downunder.

91 Bond Mark C

Small Blunder

Nowadays, when someone builds a small car it too often looks like a large one that has been thrown in the washing machine on the Too-Hot Cycle. Courageous styling has been largely forgotten. Innovative engine positioning and east–west seating have been ignored, while sub-400-cc engines have been unfairly consigned to the automotive scrapheap. Passenger doors tend to be apportioned evenly on each side of the car. Indeed, the art of designing a minicar has been transformed into a dull, clinical science.

Yet there was a glorious period in the 1940s, 1950s and early 1960s when minicar builders were in fervent competition to produce the most ridiculously proportioned small car in the world. And the British were hard to beat, with such eccentric three-wheeled conveyances as the AC Petite, Reliant Regal and Bond Mark C.

Of this unholy trinity it was the Bond that had the silliest proportions, and the oddest mechanical feature: a front wheel that could be turned 180 degrees, so that the car could swing around in almost its own length. This was a response to the loopy tax laws which classified small three-wheelers as motorcycles, as long as they didn't have a reverse gear.

The Mark C story started with the Bond Mark A in early 1949. It had an aluminium body stretched over a wooden frame, no doors, no brake on the front wheel and no rear suspension. Two years later the Mark B added rear suspension and even an optional electric starter instead of the usual pull-by-hand system. With the Mark C, from 1953, Bond discarded the cigar-shaped nose in favour of a conventional automotive front-end with integral headlights. This new nose included flamboyant front guards, presumably to convince people – very unobservant people – that the Bond was a normal four-wheeler.

The Mark C also had brakes on all wheels and a weatherproof-ish hood as standard equipment. So lavish, in fact, were the Bond people feeling this time around, they even included a door, conveniently located on the opposite side to the driver.

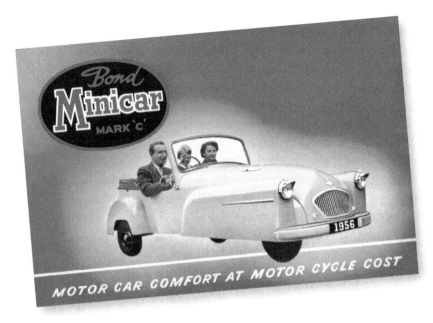

The Bond used a one-cylinder 197-cc, 6-kW engine to light up the single front crossply (via a chain), and the body panels were made of fibreglass, aluminium or steel, depending on the mood of the factory foreman on the day it was built. The shape of the rear guards were quite different on each side of the car.

The Mark C had an outrageously long bonnet, leaving the occupants all crammed at one end. The front bench seat was advertised as being suitable for carrying two adults with a child in the centre, while Bond claimed the inward-facing rear seats on the Family Safety Model could accommodate two children 'in complete safety'. These seats were in fact cantilevered over the rear axle in an area now commonly referred to as the crumple zone. Another major selling point was upholstery made from 'best quality Red Vynide'. This gave the Bond a huge advantage, no doubt, over those cheapskate competitors using second-rate Red Vynide.

A 1955 brochure claimed the Mark C was the 'only car built on aircraft principles' but failed to mention which aircraft principles these were. The brochure also took the liberty of quoting Stirling Moss, who had won the British Grand Prix of that year. Moss said the 180-degree steering was very effective, the controls were in easy reach and the ride comfort was surprisingly good. Strangely though, he failed to make any comments regarding the roadholding or handling other than to say 'it is of course inadvisable to use too much [steering] lock when travelling at a fast speed'.

'It's got everything,' boasted the brochure, next to a photo of a vehicle with, well, nothing. One of the many things the Mark C lacked was a speedometer. Thanks to the open cockpit, however, Bond drivers could easily yell out to other motorists to ask how fast they were going – as long as those other motorists were still stuck in first gear.

92 Lada 110

The Poorsche

After punishing the Russian people and a few foreigners for more than a decade with the dire and distressing Lada Samara (also known as 'the 1300', 'the Volonte', and 'the cause of the blockage'), the pioneers of Total Quality Mismanagement and Not-Quite-in-Time production supplemented it with an all-new model.

It was the Lada 110, first shown in 1995. Lada claimed to have incorporated design suggestions from Porsche. The head aches trying to imagine what these suggestions might have been.

To many car buyers, the sign of quality is a car with doors that shut with a resounding *clunk*. In keeping with the quality Lada buyers expected, the 110 had doors that opened with a resounding *clunk*.

93 Tatra Electronic

Fancy a Spin?

The Tatra T613-4 'Electronic' was displayed at the 1993 Frankfurt Motor Show. The sight produced mixed emotions, though many were happy to see the return to the West of a brand with an exceptionally long and illustrious history.

It was soon after the First World War that the eccentric genius Hans Ledwinka built the first of what was to be a long line of Tatra cars. In 1931 the first rear-engined model was seen, and in 1934 the company introduced an air-cooled V8. During that same decade Tatra produced some of the most aerodynamic bodies on the road and built vehicles as varied as a limousine with a 6.0-litre V12 and a 528-cc three-wheeler.

When the Western powers so generously gave Czechoslovakia to Hitler just before the Second World War, the newly installed German officials commandeered local cars – and showed a marked preference for the luxurious Tatras. However, it is said the Germans had so many accidents in these big and unorthodox rear-engined Tatras that a general edict was issued prohibiting their use by any member of the occupying forces.

After the war the Marxist government nationalised the plant and insisted the company concentrate on trucks and railway carriages. It would build only as many cars as was necessary to spirit party officials around. Tatra continued to do things differently, however. Indeed, it was perhaps the only car maker in Eastern Europe that remained innovative and interesting throughout the Communist years, building rear-engined V8 saloons rather than two-stroke economy cars, or those strange retro-Americana limousines favoured by Politburo members. It did so, however, with ever-decreasing production numbers.

While the fall of the Berlin Wall suddenly opened huge new markets to companies such as Tatra, it also highlighted the vast gulf between automotive East and West. The Tatra T613-4 seen at the Frankfurt show was sitting among a new crop of Benzes and BMWs that were as modern under the surface as they were above it. In contrast, the Czech machine had a 1960s body hiding mechanical attributes that went back a lot further than that.

The two 1993 models were specially developed for the West, though both were 'fourth generation' variants on the venerable T613 sedan. With a body designed in Italy in 1968 (the first to be styled outside the Tatra factory), this model was first produced in 1973. Development cycles in the old Soviet bloc were nothing too speedy or spectacular. In 1980 the first update of the T613, known as the T613-2, introduced black bumpers to replace the chrome ones. Production had peaked in the late 1970s with around 1,500 cars produced each year. By the 1980s it was a few hundred. Tatra was only just breathing when the wall came down.

The 'Electronic' variant of the T613-4 was 5 metres (16½ feet) long and weighed 1,700 kg (3,748 pounds). It was crammed with much after-the-fact whizzbangery, explained in rather tortured prose in the

English-language brochures: 'This new class-leading automobile . . . embodies all an up-to-date business-man needs . . . Intelligent self-diagnostic and audiovisual systems both speak an eloquent language. This is an ingenious merging of time-tested technology and innovative faculty of Tatra people.'

Power came from an air-cooled, direct injection 3.5-litre V8, sitting over the back axle. This engine was probably ready to be dismissed as an antique if not for the impressive 147 kW (197 bhp) and 300 Nm (64,480 lbs/ft) output. The mechanical layout, according to the brochure, represented 'the over-rear-axle engined technical conception that guarantees the perfect performance in any road-traffic regime which has, in general, been the privilege of only high-duty sports cars. Both rich-dimensioned energy-absorbing crush zones, resulting in a positive effect onto the all aboard safety are, in the event of an impact, of a great priority.'

Although the company had once built cars with handling so evil that Nazis weren't allowed to drive them, the 1990s model received generally complimentary reviews from the German motoring press. Sales, however, stayed in that uncomfortable zone between none and not very many. The story was similar in the UK, where the T613-5 was launched in 1994.

The '5' version, with a cabin heating system that could be programmed up to five days in advance, was to be the last. Just eleven cars were completed in 1996. A revamped version (described as the T700) was displayed in Prague that year but sales did not pick up. The last Tatra car was built in 1998, though plans for a revival have been regularly floated.

94 Bristol Blenheim

Old Bomber

You could possibly forgive a four-speed transmission, solid rear axle, pushrod engine, separate chassis, and general dearth of modern technology in a twenty-first-century car if that car was extremely cheap or looked drop-dead gorgeous. But what if it cost a motza (a great amount) and looked like a 1970s Ford Capri coupé suffering from water retention?

That's the question one has to ask when confronted with the Bristol Blenheim, a conveyance still in production in the new century and priced as we go to press at something exceeding £140,000. Yes, do not adjust your book. That price was £140,000.

The Bristol Blenheim takes its first name from the city in which it is built and its second from a Second World War fighter-bomber from the days when Bristol was a major aviation manufacturer. Which was a very long time ago. After the Second World War, with something of a slump in aircraft demand, Bristol took the same route as Messerschmitt and others: it turned to cars. To ease the transformation, Bristol bought licences from BMW and produced its own versions of these German cars in the United Kingdom.

Bristol Cars had some success at Le Mans in the early 1950s, and from the very early 1960s the brand was in the hands of a former racing driver named Tony Crook. Under his leadership, the 1960s and

1970s brought a series of Chrysler-engined cars, some with aviation-themed names such as Beaufighter and Brigand. The Blenheim coupé's flat-sided, oddly proportioned shape goes back to the Bristol 603 model of the mid-1970s, though it seems the name Blenheim wasn't used until the 1990s.

The official production estimate for the Blenheim is 'no more than 150 per year', though an independent estimate put it perhaps more realistically at 'about two', No outsiders are allowed to visit the factory where the cars are banged together – sorry, hand-crafted – because the workers are supposedly also involved in secret design work for the aviation industry. It is to be hoped that this work is a little more up to date than anything they are doing with road vehicles.

But back to the appearance of the Blenheim car. The official literature avoids terms such as 'porky piece of 1970s excess', preferring the more reassuring affirmation that the appearance 'is

carefully tailored to achieve quiet understatement yet maintain an elegant, timeless line'. It also says the Blenheim (the product, it adds, of the only luxury-car maker under British control) takes three to four times as much labour to build as other luxury cars and is a 'true gentleman's Grand Touring coupé – favoured by the most skilled and enthusiastic drivers'.

'In a Bristol,' we are told, 'every journey becomes an occasion, a relaxing and satisfying place from which to observe the hectic world without.'

Inside are the usual British luxury accoutrements, including soft leather seats, thick carpets, and slabs of walnut veneer, though assembled with 1960s and 1970s construction techniques and design sensibilities. To save cost the Blenheim incorporates many off-the-shelf components such as Vauxhall rear-light clusters, while beneath that 1970s body is pure 1950s technology. There's a huge separate chassis under a hand-beaten aluminium skin. This soft and expensive aluminium doesn't result in particularly light weight, though. The Blenheim weighs nearly 2 tonnes, despite being a comparatively modest 4.87 metres (16½ feet) long.

The engine, a 5.9-litre V8 borrowed from Chrysler, is also ye olde worlde. A four-speed auto box is standard, and a dual-fuel engine (gas and liquefied petroleum gas, or LPG) was offered circa 2003 to reduce running costs and improve emissions.

Electronics? Not many. Bristol claims its own mechanical brake-assist system, say, gets along very well without the need for any nancy-pantsy computer-controlled antilock overrides. A stability control system? Yeah, sure. It's called the steering wheel.

The claimed performance is 0-to-60 mph in a sprightly 6.3 seconds, but this and claims of outstanding aerodynamics, stupendous refinement, and stunning performance have been hard to verify, since members of the press are not given access to evaluation vehicles. Well, they might give away secrets to Jerry, old boy.

95 Nissan Pulsar EXA

Turbo Less Than Terrific

Renault's Formula One exploits made turbocharging the automotive craze of the early 1980s. In a world recovering from an energy crisis and still thumbing its nose at large capacity engines, turbocharging seemed a magical solution: startling performance if you wanted it, but winning economy if you drove gently. The reality was a little different, but the public's romance with all things forcibly inducted was to last several years and drag in most major road car manufacturers.

It was Nissan that was first to fully capitalise at the lower end of the market. It unveiled the EXA Turbo coupé in late 1982. Confused at the time as to whether its cars were called Nissan or Datsun, the company gave the EXA a plethora of signage that covered either outcome, plus

a Pulsar badge or two for good measure. However, all were out-shone by the large and bright 'Turbo' stickers that dominated the EXA's bodywork and trim. Even the seats had 'TURBO' crocheted into their pattern.

The EXA's generous allocation of problems started on the outside – the person who styled the front appears to have never talked to the designer who did the rear, and the structural rigidity engineer was trapped in the lift. Never mind the looks or quality, Nissan seemed to be stressing, *feel the turbo.*

The EXA used a tarted-up version of the everyday Pulsar hatchback's 1.5-litre four-cylinder engine, fitted with fuel injection and turbocharger. On most markets the EXA cost less than half the price of the next cheapest turbo sports model (the Mitsubishi Starion) and a small fraction of any 'blown' Porsche or Lotus.

One novel feature was automatic lane-changing. This was effected by pushing the accelerator. Nothing much happened until the rev counter reached 3,000 rpm, when suddenly the front end lit up and the steering wheel performed a waltz no matter how hard you held it. You could also play the Lane Guessing Game under braking; alternatively, you could throw the little EXA into a corner and take bets on whether you'd experience gross understeer, supreme understeer or terminal understeer.

For all that – and the real risk of turbo meltdown if you turned off the engine immediately after hard driving – the EXA boasted a relatively modest 77 kW (101 bhp) and 157 Nm. And the performance, thought to forgive all other sins, would be bettered by most modern family saloon cars.

96 Alfa Romeo Montreal

Neurotic Exotic

As the 1960s turned into the 1970s, Alfa Romeo was a company in crisis. So nothing out of the ordinary there.

On this occasion the confusion and upheaval was due to a surprise decision to build an entirely new high-volume small car (the Alfasud) in an entirely new factory in Naples, rather than the traditional home of Alfa, Milan. This precipitated a bizarre form of industrial warfare between Alfa workers in the north and south.

And if that wasn't enough, amid the rushed and fraught development of what was to be its smallest, cheapest car, the company decided to simultaneously develop the most expensive and complicated car in its history. On mature reflection, it might have been just a bit too much.

The newcomer was based on a Bertone-designed coupé presented at Expo '67 in Montreal (hence the un-Italian name), though the official announcement of the production version didn't come until March 1970. Even then, it was another a year before any finished examples rolled off the end of the line, thanks to strikes at Bertone's body factory.

That the Montreal looked spectacular was never a point of argument, even if the mid-engined poise was all smoke and mirrors (the engine was in the nose; those big vents behind the doors had nothing to do with cooling the powerplant). The Montreal introduced Alfa Romeo's first ever V8 for the street (pre-war Alfa eights had an inline configuration), in the form of a downsized version of the company's famous 3.0-litre racing engine. This was an all-alloy, 2.6 litre, quad-cam, 16-valve, dry-sumped donk with mechanical fuel-injection.

If nothing else, the engine was a triumph of compactness. Most Italian car makers needed twelve cylinders to fit in as much complexity and temperamental character as Alfa had managed with eight. It drove through a five-speed ZF manual floor shift. Or didn't, if the mood took it.

In June 1972, *Motor* magazine announced that right-hand drive versions would be in the UK shortly. The word 'shortly' means different things to different people. Although well-heeled British Alfaholics had signed up for Montreals when a right-hand drive prototype was shown at Earls Court in October 1971, it would be almost three years before the factory 'right hookers' finally arrived. The never-ending delays even prompted some keen buyers to have left-hand drive cars privately converted.

If considered a fully fledged Italian supercar, the Montreal was competitively priced at around £5,000, though it was hard to work out why anyone (other than a one-eyed Alfista) wouldn't go for the faster Ferrari Dino at just £222 more.

The Montreal had exotic features such as power-assisted ventilated discs front and rear. But it was softly sprung with lots of body roll, and had a tail with a tendency to jump around (strangely, the exotic engine put its power down through an old-fashioned solid rear

axle). And boy, every foible of Alfa ergonomics was there in abundance, with poor vision, lousy ventilation, a driving position that could be adjusted between uncomfortable and very uncomfortable, and a dated dashboard with a layout that defied any normal conventions of utility. The instruments were hard to read and the pedals infuriatingly badly positioned, while the rear seats provided exactly zero legroom.

Reliability and durability were, alas, everything you'd expect; indeed there are some of us who maintain that at Alfa Romeo in the 1970s and 1980s the CEO reported to the spare parts manager. And then there was the battle the owners had yet to fight: with rust.

Of a total production run of almost 4,000, fewer than 200 were built in right-hand drive. Production finished in 1975, but it would take a couple more years to push the last examples off Alfa showroom floors.

97 Isuzu Minx PH10

Bad to Worse

In the early 1950s the Japanese deserved their reputation as makers of rotten little cars with little to commend them. After all, they were mostly building British and French automobiles that perfectly matched that description.

Not only that, the emerging Japanese car makers were doing it with low technology (even by the standards of the cash-strapped post-war European industry), and in undercapitalised factories which often had dirt floors and were staffed by strike-prone employees who possessed little or no experience in the motor industry.

Soon after the Second World War, Japan's all-powerful industrial body MITI had demanded an indigenous motor industry. To this end it produced legislation which would effectively end the importing of cars from 1952. However, MITI knew local car makers had to do an apprenticeship, so suggested they start assembling the latest small Euro cars (more suitable for Japanese roads than US cars, and cheaper), while a components industry was developed that would allow full local manufacture.

The result was such curio-atrocities as the Isuzu version of the Hillman Minx and an equally loathsome series of Datsun-built Austins from Nissan. During the same period, a string of horrendously ugly and unstable locally conceived passenger cars also appeared.

Anglo-autophilia was nothing new in Japan. In 1918, a corporate ancestor of Isuzu signed a deal to produce Wolseley cars. Nissan built a version of the Austin 7 in Japan before the war, and produced the A40 under an official agreement with Austin from 1952.

Nissan was an unhappy place at the time. It was dogged by strikes and several times it tottered on the edge of bankruptcy. Yet through most of the 1950s, Nissan-Austins were the best-selling cars in Japan, with the company's production topping 20,000 for the first time in 1957.

Hino (the bankrupt carcass of which would later be absorbed into Toyota) opted to produce Renaults. As built in Japan between 1953

and 1961, these rear-engined French machines quickly gained a reputation for breaking up on country roads. In the same year that Hino took the Gallic route, Isuzu struck its deal with the Rootes Group to produce Hillmans. Isuzu had produced a small number of cars before and after the Second World War, but commercial vehicles had mostly been the mainstay of the company.

The 1953 Isuzu Minx PH10 model had a 1.4-litre side-valve engine developing around 32 kW (43 bhp) at 4,400 rpm. By 1957 the Minx was entirely manufactured in Japan, though its sales lagged well behind that of Nissan's Austins.

When rendered with the Japanese technology of the 1950s, the Minx was even heavier, slower and less refined than the original. Similarly, Nissan's Austins gave little hint that we would soon see an automotive juggernaut in the East, a country producing cars so well-finished, well-equipped and refined they would force European and American manufacturers to completely reassess the way they designed, built and marketed their cars.

And for all their faults, there was a pay-off with those early Japanese copy-cars. Although they were crude and heavy, most were also rugged. This was thanks partly to over-engineering and, as the 1950s progressed, to improvements made to the original designs by fast-learning Japanese engineers. When two Austin-based Datsun Bluebird 1000s were sent to compete in the 1958 Mobilgas Around-Australia Trial, they showed themselves better able to handle rough Australian roads than the original donor cars. One scored a class win. Yes, it was in a class with little competition, but the feat caused huge pride in Japan.

From there things moved quickly. In 1959 Nissan produced its first truly home-grown Bluebird and in 1961 Isuzu produced the Bellel. It was a four-door saloon that looked remarkably like an Austin but was claimed as an original production. Greater success came for Isuzu with the Bellett of 1963, by which time the Japanese were less interested in praising Hillmans and other British cars than burying them. It is a mission now pretty well complete.

98 Austin X6

The Pre-76

Claimed as the most advanced family car ever built in Australia, which was not exactly a big boast, the X6 replaced the 1800 'land-crab' in 1970.

Available in Tasman form or as the more upmarket Kimberley model, the X6 was front-wheel drive with a 2.2-litre OHC in-line six-cylinder engine shoehorned 'east–west' under the bonnet. This pioneering arrangement required a separate electric fan, another rarity for the era.

There was also full-flow ventilation, newfangled hazard lights (later to be popularly known as 'park-anywhere lights') and a variety of other fancy features. The enigmatic styling was local too. Crisp and clean from some angles, from others it had an almost rear-engined Eastern European look. Output was 76 kW (100 bhp) in the one-carb Tasman and 86 kW (113 bhp) in the twin-carb Kimberley. Either could be had with a four-speed manual or three-speed automatic transmission. Handling was fairly impressive, so was the ride.

Liking it so far? Well, now the bad news. Although smaller than its six-cylinder competitors (shoulder room was especially tight), the X6 was no cheaper to run. It was particularly heavy on fuel yet lacked the low-down torque that made the Aussie big sixes so effortless to drive. And on a marketing level, British-oriented family car-buyers still

considered there to be something a bit weird and Continental about front-wheel drive.

The seats were poor (seat comfort had been a strong point of the 1800), and the X6 had a duff cable-operated gear-change, controls and switches that worked slowly or refused altogether, and wipers that didn't sweep the whole screen. Oh, and hard-to-reach switches, poorly positioned pedals, steering that was heavy and kicked back savagely and suspension which went thump in the night and day. To add to all this, there was grim build quality and miserable reliability. The X6 tended to stall at idle, overheat or just refuse to work.

In June 1972, Mark II versions of the X6 twins brought many much-needed minor improvements. Unfortunately though, the new versions failed to bring any of the much-needed major improvements. The end was swift.

99 Isetta 300

Unstable Iso Tips

Iso was a fridge maker, which probably explains the front-end of the oddball Isetta microcar the company unveiled in Turin in 1953. Designed so the vehicle could be parked nose-to-kerb and the driver and passenger could hop straight out on to the footpath, the large and heavy side-hinged front door tended to jam shut with any of the little nudges that form part of all Italian parking manoeuvres.

'Not a problem,' an Iso official explained at the launch, 'a fabric sunroof has been deliberately included so the driver and passenger can climb out.'

It was an uninspiring beginning and the ludicrous proportions of the new model – just 2.28 metres (89.9 inches) long and 1.38 metres (54.3 inches) wide – may have suggested that Iso's owner, Renzo Rivolta, should have gone back to developing a new frost-free instead. In reality, Rivolta's strange little car was eventually built in Germany, Britain, Spain, Belgium, France and Brazil as well as in Italy, and would soon have a prestigious BMW badge on its nose.

He may have started with a car that was so small it was a choking hazard, but Renzo Rivolta was far keener on developing a large and exotic sports car, which he courageously wanted to call the 'Iso Rivolta'. He thought he could finance the Rivolta by licensing someone else to build the Isetta. First he manufactured about 1,000 Isettas in

Italy, then found a willing partner in BMW, which bought all the Isetta tooling and shipped it to Germany. BMW started manufacturing its version from 1955.

The original Isetta was powered by a two-cylinder, two-stroke motor scooter engine, with a chain driving a pair of closely spaced rear wheels. BMW swapped this powerplant for one of its own single-

cylinder four-stroke motorcycle engines, first a 250 mL version then a 300 mL. This made it less noisy and smoky, if not a vast amount quicker. As with the original, the BMW version had the steering wheel and instrument panel attached to the front door so they swung out of the way when people entered or exited.

BMW's brochures showed a child sitting between two adults on the rock-hard front bench seat. The company also boasted the export versions had air-conditioning, though, as if to prove it was no more a luxury car than it was a three-seater; this turned out to be merely a grille in the outer door panel that allowed air to come in.

In Germany the littlest BMW was quickly dubbed the rolling egg, but in English-speaking markets Isettas (and their ilk) became known as bubble cars.

From 1957, the Isetta was built in Brighton, England, by Dunsfold Tools under licence to BMW. The door was hinged on the other side so the steering wheel could be put on the right, but this led to a new problem. In the original left-hand drive version, the driver and engine balanced each other out. The British version had them both on the right side of the car, requiring a counterweight on the left. The handling that resulted, according to the *Motor*, was quite different in left-hand and right-hand turns.

Of the shrieking engine noise within the cabin, the *Motor* said rather politely that 'an air-cooled motor in close proximity to the rather confined interior inevitably produces more noise than the motorist is used to'. The magazine also recommended owners turn off the fuel tap on the parcel shelf if the car was to be stationary for more than a few minutes. A sophisticated vehicle it wasn't.

The UK manufacturer, soon renamed Isetta of Great Britain Ltd, produced an even weirder three-wheeled version. Having one less wheel greatly reduced the purchase tax, more than halved the annual licence fee and enabled the Isetta to be driven by a sixteen-year-old with a motorcycle licence. It also made it even less stable, but drivers could think of the money they were saving as they slid, tripped, crashed and burned.

The three-wheeler had other quirks. The reversing gear was disconnected (to comply with the lower tax rules) and, with its large 9.1-metre (30-feet) turning circle, owners often needed to jump out and manually shift the tail. Fortunately the weight was just 355 kg (around 783 pounds).

Strangely, although made in Britain for Britain, the three-wheeler was available only in left-hand drive because even the counterweight system wasn't enough to keep it anything even approaching stable.

About 200,000 Isettas were sold around the world before production petered out in the early 1960s.

100 Panther Rio

Crewed Effort

Panther Westwinds Ltd built its first model in the early 1970s, inspired by the Jaguar SS100 of the 1930s. The second Panther looked like the monstrous Bugatti Royale limousine of the same era.

In 1975, however, Panther completely changed tack and built the truly bizarre Rio. Conceived as a miniature Rolls-Royce, right down to the Parthenon radiator grille, the Rio was intended to lure traditional buyers of the Flying Lady-adorned cars from Crewe. It was reasoned they would need something more economical during the era's oil crisis and general financial meltdown.

On the plus side of the ledger, the Rio was half the price of the vehicle it aspired to be. On the debit, it was three times the price of the car it really was: a four-cylinder Triumph Dolomite.

Why anybody would base anything on a Dolomite, let alone a luxury car with a hand-beaten aluminium outer skin, was a question almost too scary to ask. Jankel believed the little Triumph's very upright seating position was consistent with the limousine ambience he was aiming for. To further assist in creating a Roycely ambience, the interior trim was all Connolly hide with contrasting leather piping, the doors and dash had burr walnut capping, and there was a big built-up centre console. Electric windows were fitted all round and each passenger had an ashtray with cigar lighter. There were even little Union Jacks on the door sills.

Unfortunately, the Rio's plusher trim intruded further on the Dolomite's limited interior room and reduced what was already marginal headroom. And when the air-conditioning was fitted (it was an option), there was no normal ventilation system. You could be too cold, use only the heater and be too hot, or choke. No tester found the middle ground. And if all four passengers were using their personal ashtrays and cigar lighters, the state of the air in Rio would be almost too horrible to contemplate.

Two versions were offered: an '850' based on the standard Dolomite, and the Especial, based on the 2-litre Dolomite Sprint. The Especial's loopy list price of £9,445 made it dearer than a Jaguar V12 saloon or a Mercedes 350SE. The brochure boasted the Rio brought 'hand-crafted exclusivity without ostentation', though why Panther thought a typical Rolls-Royce owner would want something without ostentation is hard to grasp.

Large amounts of soundproofing stifled the worst noises of the Triumph engine, but this soundproofing also added weight, which made the steering pig heavy and slowed the whole package down. Even with the premium model, 0 to 60 mph took a bit under 10 seconds, which was nothing too Especial. This was about a second and a half slower than a standard Dolomite Sprint, though Panther claimed it was still comparable with a Rolls-Royce Silver Shadow.

Using the Dolomite as the base meant the Rio maintained that model's harsh gear-change and heavy clutch (the Rio was a manual-only proposition), and it inherited iffy Triumph reliability. Well, actually there was nothing iffy about Triumph's Dolomite. You knew it was going to break down.

Just thirty-eight Rios were built. Or, to put it another way: despite everything you've just read, as many as thirty-eight Rios were built.

101 Citroën Ami 6

The Unmentionable

It is said that Flaminio Bertoni, the brilliant sculptor and designer responsible for the shape of the landmark Citroën DS, considered the Ami 6 to be his finest achievement. Which leads to some interesting questions, such as 'why?'

To most people the Ami 6 was one of the most ungainly cars ever built, with almost nothing to commend it from nose (a mess of curves and oblongs) to tail (weird-as reverse rake windscreen, strangely creased boot-lid, tiny tail-lights).

The Ami 6 was launched in 1961. It was based on the 2CV platform and widely known as the 3CV, or that 'ugly thing over there'. Not even Britain's ever-so polite *Motor* could quite hide its dislike, saying in a 1962 report that the Ami 6 had 'some features that are most commendably unorthodox and others that seem to be quite pointlessly different from what most people have found satisfactory'. Other comments in the same report suggest the ugliness was more than skin deep. The test car, for example, had an engine 'that vibrates considerably at some speeds and is decidedly noisy at others'.

Despite everything, the Ami 6 went on to become the biggest-selling car in France for the year of 1966, and by the time production ended in 1969, about 1 million had been built. Significantly, the majority of these were the less hideous estate, or Break, version.

An English-language brochure from 1965 opens with the words, 'In the forest, the branches of the trees catch the rays of the sun, and the pine-needles gently shimmer in the evening light; down and beyond, the waves softly lap the sea-shore.' As you can see, they decided it was best not to mention the car.

102* Trabant P601

Workers' Triumph

The widely held belief that the bodywork of the East German Trabant was reinforced with cardboard was a vicious lie spread by anti-revolutionary forces in the pay of running dog capitalists. There was no cardboard in the body of the glorious people's car of the German Democratic Republic. To strengthen its Duraplast outer panels, the Trabant's makers used nothing less than genuine cotton fibre.

The Trabi – as it became commonly known – was much more than an automobile. It was a subject of derision, an environmental disaster, a danger to those inside and out, and an international declaration that Communism didn't work.

Ironically, the eastern parts of Germany had a fine tradition of car building. Before the Second World War, the Horch luxury brand, which was part of the Auto Union concern, was produced in the same Zwickau factories that later disgorged the Trabant. Unfortunately, when the East German workers seized control of the means of production after the war, automotive standards quickly slipped behind those on the other side of the divide.

The Trabi was the product of the Sachsenring company, which, after producing tractors and trucks during the late 1940s, turned to

---

* Special extra Naff Motor at no extra cost but only while stocks last.

making cars based on pre-war designs from the DKW company. These had front-mounted two-stroke engines and – by the mid-1950s – bodywork made from Duraplast. This cotton fibre-reinforced resin was cheaper and easier to come by than steel (which the military had first dibs on anyway). And, unlike fibreglass, it could be shaped in a press and didn't need to be painted, as long as you were happy with a finish like that of a Bakelite radio.

Sachsenring's P70 model, unveiled amid government-approved levels of excitement at the 1955 Leipzig Industry Exhibition, captured the essential ingredients of the later Trabant; indeed, a slightly smaller version produced from 1957, the P50, was the first vehicle to use the Trabant name.

The Trabant P50 represented car-making at its most basic but could transport four adults in discomfort. It mutated into the P60; then in 1964 a major reskinning produced the longest-running and best-known Trabant, the P601 model.

The Trabant P601 was not a complete disaster from day one. There were economy cars on this side of the divide that were very similar – the Goggomobil sedan, for example. But the likes of Goggomobil knew when to throw in the towel. The Trabi P601, however, kept going for nearly thirty years and became internationally infamous when thousands of them noisily spluttered through the ruins of the Berlin Wall in 1989.

The P601 was powered by a 600-cc (36.5-cubic-inch) two-stroke twin, which was air-cooled for lower cost and higher noise. The bodywork looked like a child's drawing of a Triumph Herald, itself several years old by 1964 and no masterpiece.

The Trabi P601 had a big door on each side that never looked properly closed, and silly little fins on the tail, even with the station wagon version. But what was it like to drive? Crap, actually. It was noisy, smoky, smelly, and rattly, with shocking brakes, dire performance, miserable handling, and a 6-volt electrical system so dismal you almost needed a torch to see if the headlights were on.

However, improvements were made in ensuing years, transforming the Trabi from a primitive, badly built Eastern Bloc deathtrap into a primitive, badly built Eastern Bloc deathtrap with a 12-volt electrical system.

Despite the odiousness of the styling, mechanical attributes, and build quality, Trabants were exported in small numbers even to non-Communist countries from the 1960s.

In the late 1980s, glasnost and perestroika opened the door for an agreement to be reached for VW to supply 1.1-litre four-stroke Polo engines for an improved 1988 version of the P601. When Communism collapsed soon afterward, the two-stroke was phased out completely and only Polo-engined models were built. Not that anyone much wanted them; with the disappearance of restrictions on what they could buy, people from the East quickly turned their backs on Duraplast and tail fins. Production finally ground to a halt in 1991.

A little later in the 1990s the car became positively trendy as a retro-chic symbol of the old East. Working and non-working examples turned up as everything from highly decorated weekend runabouts to components of conceptual artworks.